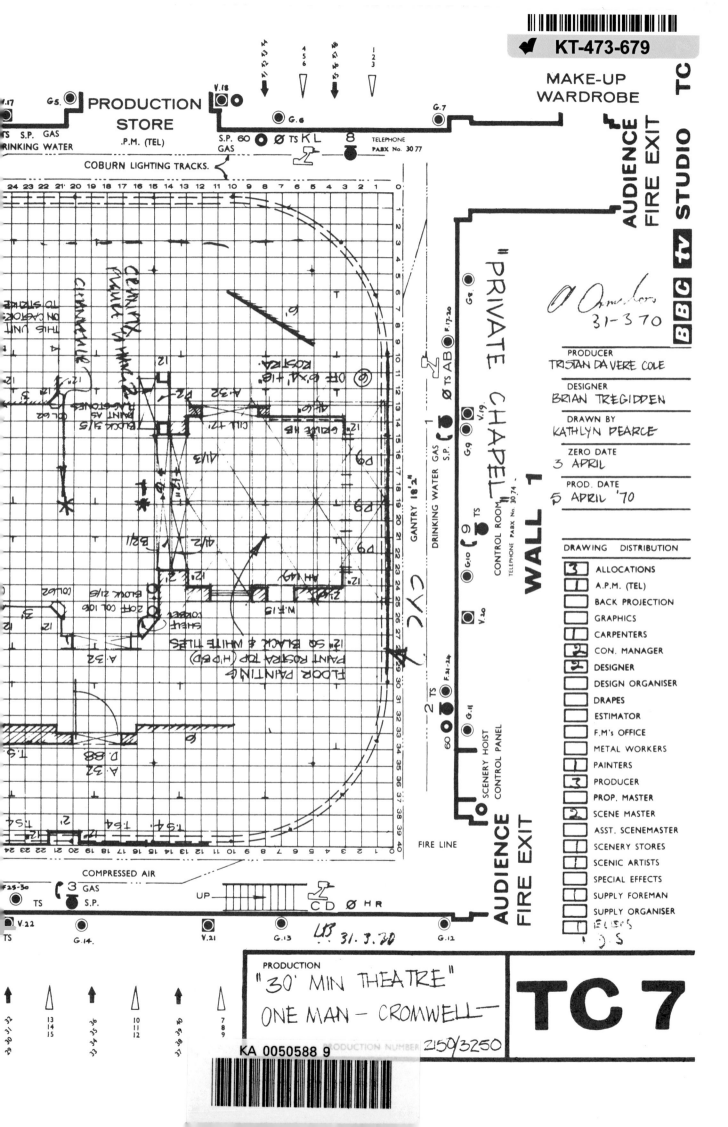

MAKING A TELEVISION PLAY

MAKING A TELEVISION PLAY

A Complete Guide from Conception
to B.B.C. Production

Based on the making of the play
CHARLES AND CROMWELL
for B.B.C. 'Thirty Minute Theatre'

by
Cecil P. Taylor

ORIEL PRESS

Published by
Oriel Press Limited
at 32 Ridley Place, Newcastle upon Tyne, England, NE1 8LH
Text set in Garamond 12 on 14 point
Printed by Knight and Forster Ltd, Leeds.

For my children

AVRAM, CLARE, DAVID and CATHRYN

ACKNOWLEDGEMENT

The author and publisher gratefully acknowledge the help and generous cooperation of the British Broadcasting Corporation which has made the book possible. Scripts, photographs, sketches, letters and diagrams are all reproduced by kind permission of the BBC. Our thanks go to all who took part in the production of CHARLES AND CROMWELL, and especially to the Producer, Innes Lloyd, the Director, Tristan de Vere Cole, and the Script Editor, Derek Hoddinott who has also participated in the production of this book.

CONTENTS

INTRODUCTION

INTRODUCTION

THE AIM OF THE BOOK

The greater part of playwriting — whether for stage, television or films — is technique. It is a craft and lends itself to the apprenticeship system of teaching, where the apprentice works with the journeyman and acquires over the years the skills of his trade.

In this book, I am throwing open my workshop to writers and others interested in the craft and giving them an opportunity of working with me through one particular job — the development and writing of a thirty minute television play.

WRITING FOR TELEVISION

One of the great problems of television at its present stage, is that it's a child trying to act like an adult. Compared to the other drama mediums, television of course, is in its infancy. At the same time, it has to compete with the other drama mediums at *their* level. Faced with competition from the other mediums and from other television companies, it's understandable that Television producers play for safety. In doing this, however, they are restricting the development of their own medium, which can only come about by vigorous experimentation at this early stage of television.

Whether those controlling the medium will recognise this and allow television — and television drama in particular — to grow up in the future is still very much in question. Writers, then, are faced with working in the medium as it is now and CROMWELL AND CHARLES was written, accepting these limitations.

The first thing a play is about — for me, at any rate — is people: their relationships to one another and to the society they live in. I start my play then, whether it's for stage, radio or television, with the people in it. This is not to say that when I'm writing for television, I don't work within the physical limitations of the medium. Obviously I don't write crowd scenes or plays with huge casts and twenty or thirty sets for a thirty minute or even ninety minute television work. But apart from those elementary and common-sense considerations, I don't let myself get bogged down with the problems of how my characters are going to move about the set, or what visual effects I'm going to exploit or even the timing of my play. My first concern is to get the people, their relationships and their story on the paper.

This, of course, does not make for economy in writing time or typing paper. (In the first version of CROMWELL AND CHARLES, I ended up with an hour script.) But this method does have the advantage of leaving me free to concentrate on what I consider to be the real problems of a play — developing their characters and telling, as coherently as I possibly can, their story.

The shaping of the script and cutting it to size and general fitting into the studio I consider are minor, mechanical problems which can be solved with a bit of sweat after the major problem of the play itself is solved.

SECTION ONE

SECTION ONE
DIARY OF THE COMMISSIONING OF THE PLAY.

DECEMBER 1968

As a socialist never knowing how one could possibly achieve a socialist revolution in Britain, I had promised myself, for years, to look in detail into several revolutions in the past, to see how they had been achieved. I believed there was something of the superman in Cromwell, Lenin and Castro that enabled them to bring about their revolutions.

If I could sell the idea of a trilogy about revolution to somebody, I would be paid for exploring territory I had long wanted to explore.

THIRTY MINUTE THEATRE had been asking me to write something for them for some time. Towards the end of December, I wrote a short outline of the central idea of the trilogy and sent it to the B.B.C.

"REVOLUTION"

Outline of three plays on revolution for
Thirty Minute Theatre

The theme of the trilogy is the role of the individual in revolution. It will look closely at three great revolutionaries — Cromwell, Lenin and Castro, during the particular turning points of their revolutions . . . The first play, I have titled, AT WINDSOR, *the second,* RETURN TO PETROGRAD *and the third* ON SIERRA MAESTRA.

(I subsequently suggested these titles were rather coy and we should get down to brass tacks by calling spades spades. The final titles were, in fact — CROMWELL AND CHARLES. LENIN. CASTRO.)

17

30th December, 1968

Dear Cecil,

    Regarding the idea "Revolution", I have discussed this with my producer whose reservations about the idea as a whole hinges on the revolutionaries that you choose and, I think, rather underlines what I mentioned to you over lunch about the problems of casting, the number of sets, and the unavailability of film that Thirty Minute Theatre has to contend with. To begin with, I am wondering whether you could very briefly outline the three revolutionaries that you intend to tackle, and the moment which either started a revolution or, alternatively, the moment which sealed its success.

There are, of course, many ways of tackling this subject and I put this to you that we could either see what happened to a famous revolutionary once he had gained power, or as I have mentioned above, at the point of the beginnings of a revolution, and as a third alternative, the success of the revolution.

I think I also mentioned to you the desirability of a direct confrontation on Thirty Minute plays, which does seem to work particularly well in this kind of format.

Yours sincerely,

Derek Hoddinott.

SCRIPT EDITOR. THIRTY MINUTE THEATRE.

In response to this letter I submitted three outlines. The outline of Cromwell and Charles read as follows:

OUTLINE

AT WINDSOR

    Both Cromwell and Charles were ready to die for their beliefs — and Charles did. Today, when there are no beliefs firmly grounded enough to die for, it's difficult to understand the psychology of heroes like Cromwell and Charles. AT WINDSOR *is about the last confrontation between Cromwell and Charles.*

    On 28th of December, Cromwell is still moving round and round in circles in his great inner debate on the fate of the king. Events had forced him to bring Charles to trial. What Cromwell could not bring himself to do, as yet, was face up to the logical conclusion of such a trial — the condemning to death of the King.

Perhaps there was something of the manic depressive in Cromwell. On the day of the play, Cromwell is facing a severe depression. Continually he asks himself, has he done everything in his power to make manifest the will of God, in respect to judgement on the king. And of course, Cromwell being Cromwell, he answers to that 'no'. He hasn't personally spoken to Charles for over a year when he had been with him and had been moved by seeing the king with his children. He has not himself confronted Charles with the true witnessing of God as seen by Cromwell. It is clearly his duty to God, and the people, and his country, to go to Windsor where the King is imprisoned and open unto him his heart — as they indeed opened their hearts to one another during their last meeting, from which Cromwell came away saying: 'There is no more upright and constant man in the three kingdoms'.

On all grounds, political, humanitarian, moral, Cromwell rejected the idea of executing the King. The weight of having to make such a decision oppressed him so much that he had stayed away deliberately from London for weeks, hoping that the situation would somehow cool and he would be able to initiate the Rule of Saints without shedding the King's blood.

In great secrecy, he goes to Windsor. Surely, if the King will listen to him calmly, he can only admit reason and justice and the will of God is on Cromwell's side.

Charles is full of grumbles. He's had a bad Xmas. No Xmas fare. Not even a Chaplain. He had to read the service himself, etc. .

Cromwell opens his heart to him. He realises how hard it must be for the King. Not to have seen his wife for over four years. His children for a year. The family to be denied the love and comfort of a father and husband . . and so on . . He goes on to use the metaphor for the family in his attempt to persuade Charles. This is not England at the time of the Tudors . . At first, a child needs the strong authority of a parent . . But when it comes to adult years . . and so on . . . So it is with England . .

But Charles is as god-obsessed as Cromwell. God has entrusted him with sovereign authority. It is his Christian duty to save the people from their folly in rejecting his divine rights of dictatorship. Both men are affronted by the other's audacity in repudiating their arguments, despite themselves, despite all the resolutions of good will both have made . . . They both grow more and more passionate in their cause — more and more violent . . Below the abstract arguments, the heroic causes, are deeper springs, neither are aware of.

Cromwell is now satisfied he has done all that God could have demanded of him to see that His justice was done on the King. It is now clear. God has given his sign. This is last of his witness against him. The King blocks the way to the Rule of Saints . . He swings, manic, against Charles, now that he has the sign.

They part, civilised. But Charles is now in no doubt of the outcome of their meeting . . .

The King goes back to play with his dogs and study his plans for the rebuilding of Whitehall.

Cromwell goes to Parliament, to give the word the Army has been waiting for: 'God has given his word. Since the power of God hath cast this upon us, I cannot but submit to Providence.'

After some correspondence on detail the trilogy was finally commissioned on 28th April, 1969.

CECIL P. TAYLOR: REVOLUTION
We should like to commission Cecil P. Taylor to write three original television plays
called "At Windsor", "Return to Petrograd" and "On Sierra Maestra", under
the main title ONE MAN. First play to be delivered 31st August, second play,
30th September, third play, 31st October . . .
                                        Copyright department . . .
My agents negotiated a fee. Contracts were signed. We were in business.

TELEVISION AS A DRAMA MEDIUM

Unlike film, which has a virtually inexhaustible range of techniques to tell its story, television — even allowing for colour — because of the size of the screen and design of the cabinet and frame of the tube, is severely restricted in the range of visual effects it can produce. Pictures, no matter what scene, because they are framed in a 21″ box, tend to look the same. Inevitably, one has the feeling with much of television drama that one has been here before.

If the playwright is going to break away from this levelling effect which tends to rob television drama of its individuality he must understand its limitations as a visual medium and exploit to the maximum the playwright's most sure technique for stamping his personality on his work — language.

Television, as it is at present, is very much the medium for language. Thus the success of Ibsen and Tchecov on television. It is also, I consider, one of the best mediums for examining at depth, human relationships. The close-up works better on telly than on film. On film it's too big. It's difficult to make the close-up seem anything but contrived. On television it's believable. It's natural. You can show your characters sweating in agony, tense with anxiety or drinking each other in, in mutual love. The less characters it deals with and the deeper the relationship it examines, the better the medium works. Two characters on the screen at the one time is ideal, three and four are possible . . Five or six are tenable. But beyond this, you are stretching the medium.

THE THIRTY MINUTE PLAY

Although the B.B.C. have used THIRTY MINUTE THEATRE as a means of introducing new writers and are to be congratulated on their concern for new writing, the thirty minute shape is probably one of the most difficult forms in television drama. A perfect or near perfect thirty minute play is even more difficult to achieve than a perfectly realised short story and that is a rare enough achievement.

The balance between having too thin and too crowded a canvas is delicate. Thirty minutes of television time can handle only so much material.

In writing CROMWELL AND CHARLES, I had to thin out several elements from the first draft to arrive at a thirty minute shape. In an early thirty minute play I wrote, I crowded an hour's material into half an hour and the result was an exhausting experience for the actors and viewers.

Ideally, a play should run its natural length, within limits, as it does in the theatre. But till we arrive at this happy state, if we ever do, the thirty minute shape will remain the most difficult of television drama forms.

SECTION TWO

SECTION TWO

FIRST STEPS

RESEARCHING THE PLAY

There are two ways of researching a play. You have a vague idea but little sense of direction. You will find what you will find and make your play out of this. Or you have a fairly clear idea of the direction your play will take and the facts you are looking for.

Although the synopsis of CROMWELL AND CHARLES was based only on a quick reading of a few key books on the English Revolution, because of the exacting form of the thirty minute play, I was determined, if at all possible, to hold to the life and death conflict between Cromwell and Charles, as the core of the play. This seemed to me the ideal shape for the *genre*.

I knew what I was looking for:

1. To find out as much as I could about the personalities and language of the characters in my play.

2. To find out if there had been a final confrontation between Charles and Cromwell or if such a confrontation was at all feasible.

3. The issues which divided the two men — both as *they* saw it and objectively, as history sees it.

4. Dates. Such as the King's arrival at Windsor. Cromwell's in London. The final speech of Cromwell in The House of Commons.

I found, in fact, virtually no evidence that Cromwell ever saw Charles again, after the break between them, occasioned by Cromwell's discovery of the King's continued duplicity. Stories and rumours do exist that such a secret meeting took place. But all evidence seems to point against them. However, I was committed to writing a thirty minute play which would show the issues of the revolution and the character clashes as clearly as possible.

I opted then to play with history. I stuck to my final meeting.

There is strong evidence for Cromwell's indecision and loss of God's guidance at this period of his life. In his own words he admits: 'I have nothing I can speak as in the name of The Lord!' Long after the final defeat of the Royalists, in the second Civil War, Cromwell stayed beseiging a comparitively unimportant strong-hold in Pontefract, which could have been easily left to some subordinate. Clearly, he did not want to return to London and become involved in the great debate on what should be done to the king. In fact, he had to be ordered home to London, before he left Pontefract.

Cromwell's relationship with Charles started well at their first meeting at Caversham, on July 4th, 1647 . . . This was after the first Civil War, when the king became a prisoner of the army. Cromwell tells Berkely:

'I have witnessed the tenderest sight that ever my eyes beheld. The meeting of Charles and his three youngest children. The King is the uprightest and most conscientious man in the three Kingdoms . . . . . I hope God will look on me according to the sincerity of my heart towards His Majesty.'

Charles, however, was not very good at people. He could not understand Cromwell's motivations and kindness to him. As Charles saw it, Cromwell was clearly after self advancement and speculated when exactly he would come out with the request for an earldom or some such honour in exchange for his kindness to the King. It troubled him so greatly, he actually sent a Major Huntington to check on Cromwell's sincerity. And Cromwell is on record as telling the Major: 'I will stand by the King if there be but ten men left to stick to him.'

These clear records of a fundamental misunderstanding from the beginning of their relationship clearly pointed to a basis for the relationship between Cromwell and Charles in my play.

There are several contemporary accounts of the king in captivity, among them a book by Thomas Herbert, his last personal attendant, and a character in the play. From this book and the other accounts I gradually built up the 'feel', the tone, of this period in Charles' life. The records of the trial of Charles, his last speech and letters give a clear light on his personality, his life style and way of thinking.

Surprisingly, I found few books on Cromwell and those I did find were extremely sketchy on his years leading to Generalship. For his character and early history, I relied to a large extent on a collection of his speeches and writings, edited by W. C. Abbott.

It seems clear that Cromwell had no illusions about the King's double-dealings. Certain of Charles' letters fell into the army's hands . . A typical letter is one to the Scots Commissioners:

TO THE SCOTS COMMISSIONERS.

You will find a cause in favour of the Independants. The forbearance I give to those who have scruples of conscience. I did it purpose to make what I send relish better with that kind of people. But if my Scots subjects will stick to me in what concerns my temporal power, I will not only expunge that clause but likewise make what declarations I shall be desired against them.

Yet Cromwell held back from the ultimate revolutionary concept of a kingdom without a king as long as possible. 'If it but have the face of authority, be it but a hare swimming over The Thames, I would take hold of it rather than let it go.'

It was the King's own obstinancy and stupidity and distorted view of reality that ultimately forced Cromwell and Parliament to put him on trial and sentence him to death.

SENTENCE ON CHARLES FIRST, JANUARY 27th, 1649
This court is in judgement and conscience satisfied that he, the said Charles Stuart, is guilty of levying war against the said Parliament and people . . . . For all which treasons and crimes this court doth adjudge that he, the said Charles Stuart, as a tyrant, traitor, murderer and public enemy to the good people of this nation, shall be put to death by the severing of his head from his body.

WORKING OUT THE PLAY

As I researched the play, I was continually thinking and re-thinking my theme and my characters, in the light of what I found, in a series of Working Notes.

FIRST WORKING NOTES

Play is in four parts. Introduction: Showing Cromwell's indecisions. How?

In his own home in London. Probably with his wife. What kind of relationship with his wife? Cromwell looking for some sign from God. Going further? Asking himself if he was not hiding behind God? Counting the signs — for and against the execution of the King.

His wife? Backing him — and not backing him. The danger Cromwell was putting himself in. Her attitude to Charles? She had met him. And liked him. Yet her respect and admiration for her husband . . The problems of riding down to Windsor. Which day, exactly? The excuse to his wife and himself for going? Going incognito . .

Two

The King at Windsor. Plotting. Writing secret letters. His resignation to his fate? Waiting. Waiting was all he could do. Nobody around him he could trust or who had any feelings for him. *Check on this.*

Three

The arrival of Cromwell at Windsor. Secretly. How secretly? The meeting of the two men. Very difficult this. Charles operating at a different level of reality than Oliver. Charles not in touch with reality at all. This needing careful thought.

Cromwell's decision that the King must die. How can I show this? His signature on the order for the trial? The death sentence?

WORK NOTES:

1. (The concept of the confrontation taking place in the chapel occurs to me for the first time.)

The meeting between Charles and Cromwell takes place in the King's private Chapel. This is the only place Cromwell could see him in safety. Was there a small chapel the King could use in Windsor? *Check.*

Setting this meeting in chapel gives us the right framework for the theme. Charles in the place he loves above all else. In God's house.

Whose side is God on? Charles has no doubt God is on his side. Has Cromwell? At the deepest level?

2. (Clarifying Cromwell's thoughts and motivations.)

Cromwell goes to Charles with no clear idea of what he is going to achieve. Looking for signs from God, yes . . But not knowing *how* he is going to deal with the King. Certainly he should clearly emphasise to the King his life is in great danger . . . Unless he climbs down absolutely . . But Charles has been told this before. Cromwell goes to Windsor, in fact, to prove himself . . To assuage the last grain of doubt that he was hiding behind God in his indecision . . Being a near-whole man, Cromwell is moved by the King's tragedy . . His separation from his wife and family . .

3. Cromwell is concerned with man-to-man communion. Charles has never experienced such a relationship in his life. He doesn't know how such things work. He gets hold, as usual, of the wrong end of the stick. Cromwell has come to him because his game is played out — miles from the truth.

4. How does the king stand? He is uneasy. He is sure there can be no legal trial of him. Yet he is a guilty man. Not because of his conduct of the civil wars but for sending Strafford, an innocent friend, to his death. This is the focus for all his guilt. So that he knows he will not die . . and yet feels he will and should . . .

5. (Relationship of King and Thomas Herbert). Thomas Herbert kindly disposed to Charles despite politics . . Yet a bore. At the time of play, they are out of friends. Charles' servant has been bribed by an army man to steal two letters from the Queen.

6. Basically what Cromwell needs is to bring the King to recognition of his sins so that he can be Saved. On two grounds the meeting goes awry — first because of Charles' difficulties in relating to people and secondly because it seems, to Cromwell, somehow Charles is aware of Cromwell's doubts. His being cut off from the light of God. Thus Cromwell and Charles are working at two different levels. Cromwell at real depths . . . Charles on superficial matters . . Thus the two men do not connect until the King begins to challenge Cromwell's vision of the witness of God against Charles, and throwing it at Cromwell that, in fact, God has witnessed against Cromwell . . Cromwell has acted *against* God . . Here he is really queering his pitch. He is pushing the question, who is on God's side. If God is not on Cromwell's side, then Cromwell's whole framework on which he has hung his life collapses. As Charles' framework would collapse, if he accepts Cromwell's witness. THEY ARE TRYING TO ARGUE EACH OTHER INTO SPIRITUAL SUICIDE.

7. The turning point will be when Cromwell feels contact with God once again. How can I show this?

8. The answer to the question above is the crucial point of the whole play. In fact, only after I had written the first draft was I able to work out what this question really meant and how I could answer it. The clue was in Cromwell's continual battle with his temper . . He was a quick-tempered man and a Christian and this was one of great personal conflicts in his life. All during the meeting with the King, Cromwell fights his temper . . Only towards the end of the play, when the King begins to read to him the Absolution or Remission of Sins . . and *forgives him, Cromwell*! does Cromwell realise his anger against the King, as a blasphemer and a man against whom God hath witnessed, is God-Given, does he succumb to his rage . . And in his rage, he 'finds' God again . .

DIALOGUE

The Playwright has no narrative device such as the novelist or short story writer has to tell his audience the thoughts and emotions lying underneath the speech of his characters. In a play, dialogue has to do several things at the one time. It has to communicate the thoughts, feelings, motivations and life-style of the characters. It has to provide information about their past, present and future, and the nature of the relationships between one another. At all times it must maintain the tension of the story the play is telling and hold the audience. Yet never, at any time, must the playwright let the audience see what he is trying to do with his dialogue. The strings of the puppets must never show. With all these functions to serve, and stresses and strains to bear, the playwright must work to his absolute limit in mastering his basic material, dialogue.

Playwriting is not improvision at the typewriter. Before I write a line of dialogue, I must have a clear idea at what direction my dialogue is going to take.

Here are my first notes for the dialogue between Charles and Cromwell.

WORKING NOTES. FIRST CONFRONTATION

Charles comes into the chapel and finds Cromwell. Cromwell on play-acting. Charles on Cromwell betraying him for Parliament. Joking on Cromwell having tested who was against the King, so that he would know whom to purge and who not to purge from Parliament. On their first meeting as children. Charles: 'You ever had the advantage of me, General'.

Cromwell will mention that he has lost a son. Tell the King plainly: Unless he agrees to terms, his life will be forfeit. But Charles is such an impossible, stubborn bastard! (In fact *he* is the man who finally pushes the revolution to its conclusion. A revolution by the default of the King.)

If I examine the first few pages of this scene as I finally realised it in detail, it may demonstrate how I carried out some of the ideas in the above and threw out some of the others.

SCENE THREE

I felt I needed a contrast between Charles' and Cromwell's style of speech. Charles, I decided, must be near flippant, at first. Treating the meeting almost as a joke. As the direction reads in the play: HE TRIES TO ASSUME A LIGHT MANNER TO BALANCE THE ADVANTAGE CROMWELL HAS OVER HIM.

I start the scene, then, with a joke by Charles.

> CHARLES: By your favour, Cromwell. Do you take holy as well as military orders in your middle years, sir?
>
> *Cromwell tries to match this light tone. But being fundamentally a grave, serious man with much on his mind at this time, he is not as adept at it as the King.*
>
> CROMWELL: I turn player, sir . . . For the safe being of us both. (*Here, I need to tell the audience the reason for this secrecy.*) If any or your attendants might choose to report our meetings, a divine would cause you less hurt than a meeting with Cromwell.

Conversation in real life does not take the form of question and answer and logical exposition. At the same time, because I was writing about real characters from history, I was restricted within certain limits in constructing my dialogue. This was one of the great problems of the trilogy. In many ways, Cromwell was clearly a logical, obvious, sensible man. At times I was pushed into predictable dialogue by the nature of Cromwell's and to some extent Charles' personality. When I am writing dialogue for characters of my own creation, of course, I am much more free to make my own connections from speech to speech, and make sure I have variety and unpredictable connections from speech to speech in my dialogue.

In this play, I solved the problem partially, by making Charles' response and attitudes to some extent unexpected. I deliberately let his thoughts move in a series of tangents.

This fitted in, too, with his character. Charles would not ask directly the question he is burning to ask — what does Cromwell want in Windsor? He was not that kind of man . . He is much more devious.

CHARLES: Sir . . I am uneasy . . If you come to talk matters of state . . . I am uneasy . . Doing this business in God's House.

In speech we have not the leisure to construct elegant, well phrased sentences or choose our words as carefully as in writing. Thus the repetition. 'I am uneasy', twice.

Then, when Cromwell answers Charles' question:

CROMWELL: Rest easy, sir. I come on God's business.

Another tangent from Charles.

CHARLES: They tell me you have been ill, General.

(This serves to knock Cromwell. He has been ill. Consequently he is in a position of weakness).

CROMWELL: It has pleased God, sir, to mend me.

CHARLES: I rejoice at this. (*He is at this point in complete control of the situation.*) Will we sit, Cromwell? (*Back to his anxiety about the nature of Cromwell's mission. But still deviously.*) Whatever business you would talk with me . . . Let us try to be easy in the talking of it.

(I am trying to create a sense of a real relationship forming between the two middle-aged men — a feeling that they are real and 'touching' one another. Charles is moved by Cromwell's presence and this feeling to talk about Cromwell's son).

CHARLES: I was grieved, Cromwell, to hear you lost a son in this sorry business. I grieved for you.

CROMWELL: (*The wound is still too raw to talk about it. Instead he hides behind the set formula of biblical language.*) The Lord giveth and the Lord taketh away. Blessed be His Name for ever and ever.

CHARLES: (*Still moved by this. Even more so, despite himself*). Amen . . Yet I was sorry for this.

(Cromwell is knocked off his balance. This is not at all the way he expected the meeting to go. Charles continues in this intimate tone).

CHARLES: When we last met at Childerley, scarce two years ago, it seemed to me we were both . . . younger men. . . . Do you feel this, Cromwell?

(Cromwell is pushed into this sad line of thought by Charles. Although he automatically throws in a 'sir' now and then in his speech, he is almost talking to himself).

CROMWELL: There is some gate, sir, a man passes through into old age. It seems to me these dark years have carried us both through this gate, sir . .

(And here Charles loses control of the situation. He can't resist connecting this line of Cromwell's with the injustices that have been done to him).

CHARLES: Meagre exercise has not helped me, Cromwell. Without hunting . . . Or Hawks . . . I walk . . But walking is not riding.

(Cromwell is moved to rebuking this self pity, by reminding Charles the reasons why he was denied these things. They are now moving into conflict).

CROMWELL: I have ridden much these past months, sir . .

(Charles is still intent on his grievances).

CHARLES: I am told so . . . . And at journey's end, you were blessed by kind welcome from your lady and your family.

(And when Cromwell says nothing to this — curbing his temper, Charles moves off at another tangent).

CHARLES: Did you have a happy Christmas, sir?

(Cromwell is anxious to get down to business. In any case Christmas is something he doesn't want to discuss with this man against whom God hath Witnessed).

CROMWELL: I come to you, sir, that every man in the three kingdoms might have a happier New Year.

(*Charles is not listening. He is intent in reciting his Christmas grievances*).

CHARLES: I had a sorry Christmas. My cook disappointed me in minced pie . . Nor was there Plum Porridge. And your Army took away my chaplain. I had to read the service appointed for the day for myself, sir . .

(*Cromwell is overwhelmed with this triviality in the face of grave, serious matters . . He delivers a sensible obvious, predictable rebuke*).

CROMWELL: I am sorry at this, sir . . Yet there are many thousands who lie buried this day from this war, who would have counted themselves blessed, to have passed this Christmas Day even as a Fast Day!

But the King is still not listening to Cromwell. Charles fancies himself as a master politician . . He has just hit on an exciting, absolutely brilliant attack on Cromwell).

CHARLES: Sir . . . I will speak open with you. You have the surprise of me. I was certain in my heart, after your last desertion of me at Childerley, I would have no sight of you again — excepting, perhaps, in some hall of Justice. Temporal or Spiritual — or Divine. Sir. You have the surprise of me, this day!

(*And with this direct attack, he has given Cromwell a lead into his own attack on Charles. From this point on, the two men are in the grip of one another. Now the control passes to Cromwell — now to Charles. But from this point on, they are on collision course*).

THE LANGUAGE OF THE PLAY

There are various contemporary records of both Cromwell's and Charles' speeches. Particularly valuable is the record of Cromwell's participation in the Putney Debates and the reports of Charles at his trial and of his Scaffold Speech.

I based the language of the play on these and other contemporary records.

Starting from the blank first page of a play never becomes any easier for me, no matter how many plays I've written. The only thing to do is to plunge in and if there is a play there, it will emerge.

I never see the first few pages as anything but a means of getting into the play. Sometimes they are viable and stay in right to the last draft; sometimes they're scrapped on the first draft or at other stages during the writing.

In CROMWELL AND CHARLES, because I ended up with a sixty-minute play in my first draft, drastic cutting and changing was needed and, in fact, I threw away virtually all of my first eighteen pages.

Here is how I saw Cromwell's relationship with his wife which in fact was a thirty minute play in itself:

ELISABETH: Yet this is the thing that troubles me, Oliver. You say, The Lord has witnessed against the King. Yet still you go to Windsor, this day.

CROMWELL: Believe me, Betty .. I have not grown callous in these war years .. Rather .. The blow that was so near our hearts . . . And the sight of such great bloodshed . . . has increased my humanity . . .

ELISABETH: How did we come to this business, dear heart!

CROMWELL: I have been praying these three months, Betty. I have had nothing I can speak of in the name of the Lord! The impatient men press for a capital charge against the King .. There is no law in such a charge ..

There is no precedent . . . Clearly, it was God's will. I take up my sword to defend the law . . . But how could it be His will that I take it up again to cut down the law? He must know if the law is cut down, there are no dykes left to hold back the flood of anarchy . . . .

ELISABETH: How did we come to this day, dear husband? From the fields of Ely . . . How did you come to this great burden. . . .

CROMWELL: (*repudiating this line of weakness*).

There is no calling God's burden 'sad' or 'heavy'. If God laid it upon us, he intended neither. He is the father of light from whom comes every good and perfect gift ..

ELISABETH: Dear heart, the life of an annointed King to hang on one man's word . . . . This is too great a burden for any man . . . God surely would not place such a thing on any man!

CROMWELL: (*impatiently, taking up his shirt, dismissing her*). Betty, I tell you I am not clear in this matter . . . I am not clear in it . . . I am beset with fleshly reasoning . . . . My own .. and the fleshly reasonings of the people round me ..

ELISABETH: (*fighting against his rejection of her*). Love .. I speak in wifely kindness to you . . . Whether it comes of the flesh or the spirit — there is no stopping it . . .

CROMWELL: Betty .. My mind moves in circles in this great matter . . . It came to me that it might be God's Will that I should go to Windsor and speak with this man .. And look into his face . . . And give him the True Witness of The Lord with my own voice . . .

ELISABETH: (*moving away from him. Recognising at last Cromwell is in the grip of a compulsion beyond her reach*). I pray to God that this thing might not rest on your head, Oliver!

CROMWELL: God's Will be done, Betty.

ELISABETH: Then may God forgive me. I pray this thing was not upon the head of my husband!

Cromwell is now in control of himself . . the dialogue with Elisabeth has clarified his motivations in going to see the King. Or, at least, so it seems to him . . He is now confident . . Arrogant in his sureness.

CROMWELL: And I rejoice at it! I do rejoice at whatever burden the Lord might heap upon my shoulders. I glory in it! My heart is full of sweet music that he has chosen me as His Servant in this thing . . . (*ELISABETH turns away at this passionate psalm and goes out . . . . CROMWELL takes up his shirt . . . He throws it down angrily . . going to the door and calling after Elisabeth:*

This is a weekday! And you do give me my sabbath shirt! I instructed you specially in this . . . I wanted no out of ordinary clothes to see the King!

He stands, impatiently in the doorway, waiting for his weekday linen.

MIX TO WINDSOR.

END OF SCENE

Another thirty minute play in its own right was the conflict between Charles and Thomas Herbert as I wrote it in the first draft.

CHARLES: Let us speak openly and plainly on the cause of your coldness . . . (*Herbert is about to protest again at this but the King rides over him.*) I gave no pledge not to receive letters from abroad. Neither to Parliament, nor to the army, nor to the Governor of this castle . . Nor to any man whatsoever, sir. Sir . .

If any man should be angry in this matter, it should be The King.

You looked into my close stool, Herbert. And studied private letters between the King and his Queen.

HERBERT: Sir . . I did not read these letters.

CHARLES: By your favour, sir. Something of them you must have certainly read. Else you would not have known they were from the Queen — as you reported to the Governor.

HERBERT: By your leave, sir . . There is no gain to be won, talking of this matter.

CHARLES: By your favour, Herbert! I would talk of it. I would not have you walking my chambers, attending me and looking upon me as a rogue, Herbert.

HERBERT: Sir . . I do not look upon you in this fashion.

CHARLES: Herbert . . You must settle in your mind. Whose horse you will ride. Whether the King's — so that when he comes to his throne again, by God's will, the King will honour you for the kindness you did to him in his captivity . . Or the army's . . . So that . . If God should decree that such a thing as the sword should prevail . . . then they will honour you for your services against the King.

HERBERT: Sir . . Nothing like this runs in my mind . .

CHARLES: You have reported the finding of these two letters to the army . . And given them over to the Governor of the Castle, sir.

HERBERT: Sir, this was my duty. I am an honest servant of my country, sir.

CHARLES: And of your King, sir?

HERBERT: Sir . . this was not a kindness to me . . To bribe my own servant to conspire against his master.

CHARLES: By your favour. I did not bribe this servant. If he was bribed, it was by officers outside this castle.

HERBERT: I am bound by my oath, sir. To report anything I might hear of plans for the King's escape.

CHARLES: Then clearly, sir . . You have chosen the horse you would ride, Herbert.

HERBERT: I am bound by my oath, sir.

CHARLES: I see, Herbert . . I have it plain, now . .

HERBERT: Sir . . I have come to love you and admire you beyond any measure, in those years I have served you.

CHARLES: Yet you would deny a man's right to receive loving and kind words from his wife?

HERBERT: I would not, sir. This I would not do, sir.

CHARLES: I have not seen my wife, Herbert, for over four years. All this time, I have neither seen her face . . nor heard her voice. Except by evocation in the words written by her pen.

This was my only touching of the other half of my soul, Herbert . . And you would deny me this comfort. You would send these private words between a man and his wife to be read in public places.

HERBERT: Sir, you are King . .

CHARLES: I thank you, sir . . for these words . . I do truly thank you . .

HERBERT: And your wife, sir, is Queen . . By this fact, all words that do pass between you, in these unlucky times, sir . . . They are public words, sir . . .

CHARLES: Clearly, Herbert . . I do see it plain, now. By these words . . . You do count me guilty of making this unlucky war and of the blood which was shed in the making of it . . . You would gather even the kind words between man and wife as matter against the criminal . . .

HERBERT: Sir . . These are matters beyond my understanding . . .

CHARLES: Herbert! You parry again! Clearly, within your understanding. Since you have chosen the horse you will ride on this journey, sir . . And spy upon your King . . and deliver his letters into the hands of his enemies . . .

HERBERT: Sir . . Not unto his enemies . . Rather . . To those who would be his friends . . .

CHARLES: If I am guilty of such horrible crimes . .of such bloodshed . . If I am the author of all these misfortunes, sir . . Then why does not God in His great Wisdom not strike me down, sir? (*Herbert turns away*.) Why does not God strike me down, Herbert?

HERBERT: Sir . . . All this is beyond my understanding . . . Who is guilty and who is not in these things . . I can see no clear road through this forest, sir . . . Believe me . . These are my true thoughts . .

CHARLES: Herbert . . This is honestly said . . I believe you . . You can see neither for the King nor for his enemies . . You will stand in the middle, Herbert . . . And be cut down by both sides!

The sixty minute play, however, was too 'warm' to cut with any objectivity. I sent off the script to the B.B.C., feeling I hadn't done too bad a job on it but prepared, as always, being the kind of insecure writer I am, to be told that I had written a load of rubbish.

BRITISH BROADCASTING CORPORATION

TELEVISION CENTRE WOOD LANE LONDON W12

TELEPHONE 01-743 8000 TELEGRAMS BROADCASTS LONDON TELEX

CABLES BROADCASTS LONDON-W1 TELEX 22182

12th August, 1969.

Dear Cecil,

Innes and I have now read Part 1 of your Trilogy 'AT WINDSOR' which we like very much. It's got all the ingredients of a good, tightly constructed half-hour play.

Naturally, as you would expect, we have one or two suggestions which I hope will be an improvement:-

(a) As you already suspect, this play goes con-siderably over length and on a rough check I estimate that it needs cutting by ten pages.

Having been through the script very carefully I think we can lose, without any damage to the script at all, pages 1 to 9 - in short, the first two scenes.

As you will see, I started to make various cuts in scene 2 but when I compared this scene with the intense conversation between Charles and Cromwell at the end of the play it really was a repetition of what Cromwell had intimated in the opening. Also, I found the scene between Charles and Elizabeth rather boring and the bit with the virginal a bit cliché (if you forgive me!).

I think it is more essential to get into the play, like opening on page 10 with perhaps two short scenes of Cromwell (a) entering the chapel and (b) his struggle through prayer to come to terms with his conscience before the arrival of Charles for their confrontation. (These to be intercut into the Charles-Herbert scene).

(b) I think the confrontation taking place, and basically it is a talk about life and death, in the chapel is very good indeed but I am somewhat perturbed by the idiom that you have used. I am perfectly prepared to accept that

it is the idiom of the time but I have my
doubts as to whether it really works for
there are some pretty complicated sentences
for the audience to work out. I am
wondering, therefore, whether you could use
a more up-to-date idiom for the play as a
whole?

I would like to know what you think of these suggestions.
If you agree, we might also have to think of a new way of
finishing. If we use still shots it does mean that we have to
go to the places concerned and take them and I can foresee a number
of problems here. Is there a possibly better ending that you
can think of? I must admit to being a little stumped about
this at the present moment but when you go through it again it
might come naturally to you.

Anyway, all in all this is a good start to what I hope is
going to be a centre-piece for our next season. Please keep
it up and I look forward to hearing from you again soon.

                        Yours sincerely,

                        Derek Hoddinott
                        Script Editor
                        THIRTY MINUTE THEATRE

C.P. Taylor Esq.,
22 Wallridge Cottages,
Matfen,
Northumberland.

By this time I had written the first draft of the second play in the trilogy, LENIN, and CROMWELL AND CHARLES was sufficiently 'cold' for me to work on with some objectivity.

In thirty minutes, clearly, all I had time for was to concentrate on the conflict between Cromwell and Charles, as the Script Editor had pointed out in his letter. Out went the first scene between Cromwell and his wife, and the first scene between Charles and Herbert.

The result was the final shape of the play. I simplified some of the language, typed out the second draft, and I had my thirty minute television play, CROMWELL AND CHARLES.

BRITISH BROADCASTING CORPORATION

TELEVISION CENTRE WOOD LANE LONDON W12

TELEPHONE 01-743 8000 TELEGRAMS BROADCASTS LONDON TELEX

CABLES BROADCASTS LONDON-W1 TELEX 22182

17th September 1969

Dear Cecil,

      Thank you for co-operating so beautifully on this first script.

      I shall now authorise the second payment and you will be hearing from our Copyright Department within the next week or two.

      I shall look forward to reading 'LENIN' and give you our views in due course.

               Yours sincerely,

               Derek Hoddinott
               Script Editor
         THIRTY MINUTE THEATRE

Cecil P. Taylor,
22 Wallridge Cottages,
Matfen,
Northumberland.

NOTE ON THE LAYOUT OF TELEVISION SCRIPTS

The final rehearsal script, as will be seen, is typed on the right half of the page only, leaving the left half free for the camera instructions.

    It is typed on one side of the paper only but in this reproduction the pages have been backed-up.

REHEARSAL SCRIPT

<u>Rehearsal **Script**</u>

<u>"THIRTY MINUTE THEATRE"</u>

<u>'ONE MAN'</u>

<u>A Trilogy by Cecil P. Taylor</u>

<u>1. 'Cromwell'</u>

<u>CAST:</u>

OLIVER CROMWELL - Fifty Years Old. As in his portrait
               by Robert Walker.

CHARLES FIRST   - Forty-nine. Portrait of him at this period
               by Edward Bower.

THOMAS HERBERT   - The King's Attendant. Probably in mid
               thirties. Can't verify his age.

OOOOOOOOOO

<u>SETS:</u>

The King's Private Chamber.
The King's Chapel.
A Corridor.

"THIRTY MINUTE THEATRE"

'ONE MAN'

A Trilogy by Cecil P. Taylor

1. 'Cromwell'

1. THE KING'S PRIVATE CHAPEL.
    WINDSOR CASTLE. DECEMBER 28TH
    1648

(CAMERA ON THE CHRIST
ON THE CRUCIFIX ON THE
ALTAR.

MOVE BACK TO SHOW THE
ALTAR, THEN THE WHOLE
CHAPEL.

HOLD ON THE DOORWAY,
AS CROMWELL ENTERS.

HE STANDS FOR A MOMENT,
THEN UNCOVERS HIS HEAD.
HE LOOKS ROUND THE
CHAPEL. HE WALKS DOWN
TO THE ALTAR AND STUDIES
THE CRUCIFIX. HE STANDS
STUDYING THE FIGURE OF
CHRIST FOR SOME TIME.
THEN HE TAKES A GRIP
OF HIMSELF.. HE TURNS
HIS BACK ON THE ALTAR
AND THE OTHER RELICS OF
PAPACY. HE THROWS HIM-
SELF ON HIS KNEES TO
PRAY)

CROMWELL: Dear God in Heaven, who searcheth our hearts and knoweth all things that lie buried in all men, You only are worthy to be feared and trusted and Your appearance patiently waited upon. You will not fail your people.

(CAMERA ON HIS FACE.
HE IS STRAINING,
FIGHTING TO REACH OUT
TO GOD)

Dear God, guide me in this thing you have put upon me, Lord. Dear God I am beset with fleshy reasoning. Help me to recover your Presence that has withdrawn from me these three months ... Dear God give me some sign, that I can speak as in Your name to this man ... Help me to accomplish that work which will be for the good of this Kingdom and all its people ...

(FADE VOICE)

2. INT.   THE KING'S PRIVATE APARTMENT

(CAMERA ON CHARLES'
ANGRY FACE. HE IS
RINGING HIS SILVER
BELL, IMPATIENTLY, FOR
HIS ATTENDANT, THOMAS
HERBERT.

HERBERT RUSHES IN AND
BOWS TO THE KING)

HERBERT: Sir?

CHARLES: Sir, I have been ringing this bell these five minutes!

HERBERT: I was with Colonel
Whichcott, sir. He called me to
him.

CHARLES: By your favour, Herbert!
If Whichcott would speak to my
attendants, he must first ask
your freedom from me, sir. I
am still King, Herbert!

   (HERBERT BOWS HIS
    APOLOGY)

Did we not appoint this after-
noon for a meeting with our
architect?

HERBERT: This we did, sir.

CHARLES: At this hour, Herbert?
Three hours after noon?

HERBERT: Mr. Webb is here, sir.
This is the business upon which
the Governor called me. The
Colonel -

CHARLES: What delays him?
There is much work to be done.
This afternoon, we are to
consider the facade of the new
palace at Whitehall.

HERBERT: Sir ... Colonel
Whichcott is entertaining Mr.
Webb. He asks your indulgence,
sir. Some divine has come from
London. He begs to see you,
sir.

CHARLES: Has Webb brought
more drawings with him?

HERBERT: He has, sir.. The
Divine waits you in the Small
Chapel, sir.

CHARLES: Have the army softened to my cause and provided me with some chaplain of the true Church, Herbert? Even the army would hold their knives in the House of God ... Think you this? Or would they have a second Thomas a' Becket?

HERBERT: The Governor begs you to see this man, sir. I am to tell you there is no matter more important to yourself and the Kingdom than that he comes upon.

CHARLES: Do you find it God's judgement on me ... That I am confined to these rooms and a stretch of terrace ... Do you?

HERBERT: The terrace is of great length, sir.

CHARLES: Truly, Herbert ... It is of great length. There is a delightful view of the Thames ... And there is much pleasure to be gained from watching the ships daily under sail. There is much pleasure to be gained from this. Herbert ... You do teach me well.. To be grateful for whatever small favours God does send me in His Mercy and Wisdom. Sir, I thank you.

HERBERT: Will you see the Divine, Sir?

CHARLES: I have sinned much in the sight of God ... Manhood brings guilt, Herbert ... And I have carried as heavy a burden of guilt as any man ... But in this business of this unlucky war ... In these charges that I did take up my sword against my people ... On all these counts, Herbert, before God, so I hold myself blameless ... If I am guilty of such horrible crimes, of such great bloodshed ... If I am the author of all England's misfortune ... Then tell me, sir ... How does God in His Great Wisdom, seeing all things in all places, ... How does God not strike me down for this, Herbert? (cont ...)

CHARLES: (cont) I am being
weighed in Heaven for other sins.
If it is God's will that I be put
to death by an unjust sentence,
then this is His Judgement
against an unjust sentence of my
own against a good friend and a
loyal counsellor ... I would not
acquit Strafford when he was
oppressed by a most unjust decree
... I gave him the King's word,
that he would lose neither life
nor name nor property, by
serving truly the King's cause ...
Yet did I inflict him with an
unjust sentence and had him done
to death ...

   (HERBERT TURNS FROM
   THIS SELF INDULGENCE ...
   THE GRIEF FOR ONE MAN
   AND THE INDIFFERENCE TO
   THE DEATHS OF THOUSANDS
   DISTURBS HIM.

   THE KING, HOWEVER,
   IS TOO BUSY ON HIS OWN
   LINE OF THOUGHT ...)

How did the Governor speak of
this Divine's business with me?

HERBERT: He would do for you,
sir, the greatest kindness any
man can do for another.

CHARLES: I will see this man ...

   (HERBERT MAKES TO
   GO WITH HIM.

   CHARLES STOPS HIM)

I will see him alone ... If he is
of the true church ... Then I
would have our prayers private ...
(cont ...)

   (HERBERT BOWS AND
   KISSES THE KING'S
   HAND)

CHARLES: (cont) Did I tell
you ever, Herbert ... I can
tell a man's loyalty by the way
he kisses my hand ...

(HERBERT HOLDS THE
DOOR OPEN FOR THE
KING.

THE KING WALKS THROUGH
THE DOORWAY)

3. INT. CHAPEL.

(CAMERA ON THE CRUCIFIX.
TRACK BACK TO SHOW
CROMWELL, STILL ON
HIS KNEES, STILL
STRUGGLING DESPERATELY
TO MAKE SOME CONTACT
WITH GOD. NOTHING IS
COMING)

CROMWELL: Dear God, if there
is some sin I have committed in
these dark years of war, that
has turned your presence from
me ... Help me to discover this
sin ... Help me to cleanse myself and stand before you, pure
and worthy of Your Presence,
once again ...

(HE BECOMES AWARE OF
SOMEONE APPROACHING
THE CHAPEL. HE
BREAKS OFF. STANDS.
HE WIPES HIS FACE
CLEAN OF THE SWEAT
OF HIS PRAYER.
STRAIGHTENS HIS
CLOTHING AND PREPARES
TO MEET HIS KING.

CHARLES ENTERS, READY
TO MEET ANY MAN BUT
CROMWELL.

HE STANDS FOR A MOMENT,
TRYING TO RALLY HIMSELF
FROM THE SHOCK OF THIS
MEETING.

CROMWELL GOES TO THE
KING. HE BOWS AND
GOING ON HIS KNEES,
KISSES THE KING'S HAND.
HE IS GREATLY MOVED
BY THE SIGHT OF CHARLES.
HE IS GREY, OLD AND
TIRED - SMALLER, IT
SEEMS, THAN AT THEIR
LAST MEETING. THE
SUFFERING IN HIS FACE
BRINGS OUT ALL THE COM-
PASSION IN CROMWELL,
DESPITE HIS PRE-
CONCEIVED ATTITUDE TO
THE KING. HE IS MORE
LOST THAN EVER.

CHARLES SMILES. HE
TRIES TO ASSUME A LIGHT
MANNER TO BALANCE THE
ADVANTAGE CROMWELL HAS
OF HIM)

CHARLES: By your favour, Cromwell!
Do you take holy as well as
military Orders in your middle
years, sir?

    (CROMWELL TRIES TO
    MATCH THE KING'S
    LIGHT TONE:)

CROMWELL: I turn player, sir,
for the safe being of us both ...
If any of your attendants might
choose to report your meetings,
a Divine would cause you less hurt
than a meeting with Cromwell.

CHARLES: Sir ... I am uneasy ...
If you come to talk matters of
state ... I am uneasy ... Doing
this business in God's House,
Cromwell.

CROMWELL: Rest easy, sir ... I
come on God's business.

(CROMWELL STUDIES THE
KING, AS HE FIRST
STUDIED THE CROSS ON
THE ALTAR ... HE
SEARCHES HIS FACE, AS
IF FOR SOME SIGN GOD
MIGHT HAVE WRITTEN ON
IT ... HE STANDS,
LEAVING THE INITIATIVE
TO THE KING)

CHARLES: They tell me you have
been ill, General.

CROMWELL: It has pleased God, sir,
to mend me ...

CHARLES: I rejoice at this.. Will
we sit, Cromwell? Whatever
business you would talk with me ...
Let us try to be easy in the
talking of it ...

(THEY BOTH SIT ... BOTH
RELIEVED TO HAVE THE
WEIGHT OFF THEIR LEGS
... TWO MIDDLE AGED
MEN, MOVING INTO OLD
AGE ...)

... I was grieved, Cromwell, to
hear you lost a son in this sorry
business ... I grieved for you ...

CROMWELL: The Lord giveth and the
Lord taketh away, Sir ... Blessed
be His Name, for ever and ever!

CHARLES: Amen ... Yet I was sorry
for this ... (cont ...)

(CHARLES LOOKS AT
CROMWELL)

CHARLES: (Cont) ... When we last
met at Childerley, scarce two
years ago ... It seemed to me we
were both ... younger men ... Do
you feel this, Cromwell?

CROMWELL: There is some gate, sir,
a man passes through into old age..
It seems these last dark years have
carried us both through this gate,
sir ...

CHARLES: Meagre exercise has not
helped me, Cromwell ... Without
hunting ... Or Hawks ... I walk ...
But walking is not riding ...

CROMWELL: I have ridden much,
these past months, sir ...

CHARLES: I am told so ...

(UNCONSCIOUSLY MOVING
INTO AN ATTACK)

... And at journey's end, you were
blessed by kind welcome from your
lady and your family ...

(CROMWELL SAYS NOTHING
AT THIS)

... Did you have a happy Xmas, sir?

CROMWELL: (AVOIDS, THE QUESTION) I
come to you, sir, that every man in
the three kingdoms might have a
happier New Year.

CHARLES: I had a sorry Xmas. My
cook disappointed me in minced
pie ... Nor was there Plum Porridge.
And your Army took away my
Chaplain ... I had to read The
Service appointed for the day for
myself, sir ...

CROMWELL: I am sorry at this,
sir ... Yet there are many
thousands who lie buried this day
from this war, who would have
counted themselves blessed, to have
passed this Xmas Day even as a
Fast Day!

        (HE STUDIES THE KING'S
         FACE AT THIS DART,
         SEARCHING FOR SOME
         SIGN OF CONTRITION.
         HE FINDS NONE ... THE
         KING HAS NOT HEARD THE
         WORDS ...)

CHARLES: Sir ... I will speak
open with you. You have the
surprise of me. I was certain my
heart, after your last desertion
of me at Childerley, I would have
no sight of you again - excepting,
perhaps, in some hall of Justice.
Temporal or Spiritual - or Divine.
Sir. You have the surprise of me
this day!

        (CROMWELL IS FURIOUS
         AT THIS CHARGE, DESPITE
         HIMSELF. YET TRYING TO
         CONTROL HIS TEMPER)

CROMWELL: By your favour, Sir! I
did ever stand firm by my words to
you at Childerley. Rather, it
seemed to me that it was you
guided by false advisers, who
moved from our agreement of these
days.

CHARLES: I have your words to me
by heart. You would hazard life
and fortune rather than the King
continue a prisoner in his own
Kingdom.

CROMWELL: These were my words, sir.

CHARLES: Then, did you stand in
the Commons, and lead the general
concert of voices against the King!

CROMWELL: The reasons for which, sir, you well know. Letters which you wrote secretly came into our hands, showing your true intentions to the Army and Parliament.

CHARLES: No, sir ... These were not the reasons you gave me at that time, for your attacks on me in The Commons ... I would remind you, of the reasons you did give me. I doubted much their sincerity. But now, with the passing of time, I see never has there been more honest words. Your attacks on the King, you told me, were a means of sounding out who was against the King in Parliament. Now, sir, I see plainly your reasons, for this sounding ... So that you might discover who were the King's men in the Commons that you might cast them out and have a Commons, enemies of the King to a man!

CROMWELL: Sir ... This purge of the Commons was not my way ... There is little law in this purging. I know this. It was not needed. God would have given His People a majority in the Commons in His own time. This thing was done, while I was in the north. I came home to it. And there was no undoing of it.

CHARLES: I believe you in this, Cromwell.

    (CHARLES IS FOLLOWING
    CROMWELL'S EYES ON THE
    ALTAR AND THE CRUCIFIX.
    UNCONSCIOUSLY, CROMWELL
    IS STARING AT THEM, AS
    HE SPEAKS)

CROMWELL: Peace is only good when we receive it at Our Father's Hand. In His time. It is dangerous to snatch it and most dangerous to go against the will of God to attain it.

CHARLES: Cromwell ... I know you do love music much ... And all beautiful things ... Do you not find beauty in the ...

(HE CATCHES HIMSELF
IN TIME ON THE WORD
'TRUE')

... Old Church.

CROMWELL: (NOT TO BE DRAWN INTO THIS) Sir ... These men who made this purge ... Though they are good and godly men ... Yet they are given to haste ... This is what brings me to Windsor ...

(HE TURNS TO THE KING,
SUMMONSING UP ALL HIS
POWER OF PERSUASION TO
CONVEY THE REALITY OF
THE DANGER TO CHARLES.
BUT AS HE CONTINUES,
HE ONLY CONFIRMS
CHARLES' READING OF
HIS WORDS AS AN ATTEMPT
TO FRIGHTEN HIM INTO
SUBMISSION BY THREATS)

... These men are impatient to take some road, sir. Even though God has shown them no road which they should take, they are impatient men. They would bring you to trial, before this New Year has yet begun.

(CHARLES JUMPS TO ARGUE
POINTS OF LAW. CROMWELL
IS ON GROUNDS HE CAN
UTTERLY DEMOLISH)

CHARLES: By your favour, sir! This thing cannot be done! There is no precedent for it. By the letter of the law, all persons charged by the law must be tried by their equals.

CROMWELL: Sir, they have already found you guilty of the charges they will lay against you. Your sentence is all that is at issue, Sir. And these men are already moving to their conclusion on this.

CHARLES: What is the process, sir? If a person is questioned without an equal? There is no law for this. And if this obstacle be overcome, by twisting the law, and he is found guilty. By what power shall judgement be given? Who shall give it? Who shall pronounce sentence on him. I ask you? Who will pronounce sentence on an annointed King, sir?

CROMWELL: They are impatient men, sir. They would have you tried and sentenced, sir. If they bring you to trial ... The judgement against you is certain. I see no other end to this thing. You will be put to death.

CHARLES: No judge will sit at such a trial, sir. All persons charged must be tried by their equals. This is the root of our law, Cromwell! They might confine me to the Tower for all my life ... As a close prisoner ... They might have me done to death by unknown assassins ... Secretly ... But bring their annointed King to trial, they may not do.

CROMWELL: Yet ... If this thing should be God's will, sir ...

CHARLES: By your favour, sir!

CROMWELL: Then God will open their eyes to such a process that would allow this thing, lawfully.

CHARLES: By your favour. There is no law for such a thing.

CROMWELL: Sir, I am not at Windsor to argue point of law! I am no lawyer to do this business! I am here to open my heart to you, and to urge you to open yours to me ... That we might search together, as two men before their Father, searching for His Truth and His Will ... Praying for His Light to enter our souls ...

(CHARLES STUDIES CROMWELL. HE RISES ... TRYING TO WORK OUT WHAT EXACTLY CROMWELL IS AFTER. CLEARLY CROMWELL IS IN A POSITION OF WEAKNESS. OTHERWISE WHY WOULD HE HAVE COME TO HIM. THIS IS THE KEY POINT? FOR CHARLES. CROMWELL NEEDS THE KING ... CHARLES STANDS, STUDYING THE CHRIST IN THE ALTAR AND THE STAINED GLASS WINDOW ABOVE ...)

... This is what brings me to Windsor, sir ... To open my heart to you ... And I pray to God that He will show you only good can come of opening your heart to me, in answer ...

(CHARLES HELPS CROMWELL WITH QUIET, SWEET REASONING)

CHARLES: ... Cromwell ... My heart has been open for any man to read, these past years ... I have done everything as a Christian and a King to bring the peace. I have offered everything for this peace. I have reserved only these conditions and terms which I could not consent to, without irreparable injury to my soul and offence to God. The breaking up of my church, which was asked of me ... I could not offer this ... And the handing over of the government of my people ... How could I offer this when God has entrusted them into my care, as their King? How could I give over the charge God put upon me, and hand over their care and government to some earthly authority. (cont ...)

CHARLES: (Cont) Cromwell ... You
know the text as good as I ...
What benefit is there to a man, if
he gains the whole world and loses
his soul?

CROMWELL: Sir ... We do all have a
body of sin and death. Only through
the Lord can we find sweet
consolation. I beg of you, sir ...
Look into your heart and see if
there is no guilt there.

   (CHARLES: THIS RESPONSE
   ONLY CONFIRMS CROMWELL'S
   WEAKNESS IN CHARLES'
   EYES ... HE MOVES TO A
   MORE OVERT ATTACK)

CHARLES: At Newport, sir, not
three months past, I treated
honestly and uprightly with Lords
and gentlemen of Parliament. We
were on a happy conclusion to that
treaty, sir. But the army was
stubborn to give up the power they
had taken by the sword, which they
would lose at the signing of the
treaty and the return of the rule
of the Law. They cut down that
tree in the planting by purging
the Commons of every man who sat
there who might vote for the treaty.

(On to next page)

CROMWELL: Sir ... Before God, I
tell you ... The time is past for
such debating ... Rather, I would
talk to you of The Witness of The
Lord. Of the Providences and
Appearances of God which I have
seen these past years ... His
Presence has been among us. Look
into the providences, sir, I beg
you! How else did we prevail,
but by the Light of God's Countenance?
Two times, did you make war on your
subject. And Two times -

CHARLES: (FURIOUS AT THIS CHARGE)
Look to the orders and proclamations,
sir! The dates of the Commissions on
both sides. You will see clearly,
if you want to see, that I raised no
army before such times as parliament
raised hostile forces against me!

CROMWELL: (CONTINUING) And two
times, did the people, by the light
of God's presence, prevail.

    (CHARLES TURNS AWAY,
     IMPATIENT AT THIS
     EVANGELISM)

Sir ... These past months you have
been at your ease ... You have had
time, to reflect and meditate. Look
into these signs. They hang so
together ... They have been so
constant and clear.

    (CHARLES CLEARLY
     BORED BY ALL THIS
     TAKES UP A PRAYER
     BOOK AND LEAFS
     THROUGH IT)

Every time I did battle with your
army against great odds. Yet every
time our cause prevailed. Clearly,
the light of God has shined upon
this cause.

CHARLES: Horses, Cromwell ...
Horses.

   (CROMWELL LOOKS AT
    THE KING, PUZZLED)

Cromwell, I have studied these
battles you would have God win
for you. And all I find, are
horses.

CROMWELL: Sir ... If you do not
recognise that God has witnessed
abundantly against you ... And if
you do not admit this witness to
the world ... Before God, I
tell you, sir ...

CHARLES: Horses, Cromwell ... this
is the only sign I find in your
great victories. Your horses were
heavier than ours, Cromwell ...
Slower ...

CROMWELL: We took what horses came
to us ...

CHARLES: The weight of your charge
overwhelmed my ranks, Cromwell.
And the skill of your men in handling
their horse. Your horse and men
were drilled with much skill. I
marvelled to see them.

   (DESPITE HIMSELF,
    CROMWELL IS PLEASED
    WITH THIS PRAISE.
    HE STANDS, RECALLING
    TO HIMSELF THE DELIGHT
    HE HAD ENJOYED IN PAST
    BATTLES)

They could fight in mass, or
separate troop ... According to the
command. To see them advancing,
knee to knee! Halting at a command ...
Wheeling ... This was a wonderful and
terrible thing to see, Cromwell!

(CROMWELL GIVING
HIMSELF A SHAKE.
GETTING BACK TO
HIS THEME)

CROMWELL: I am a farmer, sir ...
I came to soldiering in my middle
years. Who showed me these things -
but God?

CHARLES: Cromwell, I tell you ...
Your horse was a thing to marvel at!
But this was all that lay in your
victories. It was the sword. This
is the title of the sword. By which
you take the government to yourselves
by force and set up a Kingdom ruled
by the law of the sword.

   (CROMWELL DESPITE
    HIMSELF, DRAWN FROM
    THE SPIRITUAL TO THE
    TEMPORAL ARGUMENT)

CROMWELL: Sir, rather did you rule
by this law of force. You did take
all powers of government to yourself,
sir. You would have absolute
authority for the King, contrary to
the law. You would command all
money in the Kingdom, contrary to the
law, sir ...You would call and
dissolve parliaments according to
whether they would bow to your will
in these things, or oppose you.
Your abuse of the law became so great -

CHARLES: This is God's house, sir!
This is not a place to talk politics
or government!

CROMWELL: Your abuse of the law
grew so great, sir, that honest and
Godly men were forced to take up the
sword to restore the old laws to
their country ...

CHARLES: By your favour Cromwell!
T h i s is G o d ' s h o u s e!

CROMWELL: This is God's business!
This is the root of the law, sir ...
That King and Parliament do rule
jointly and in common accord ... If
you would look into your heart ...
Without fear ... Clearly ... Then
you would see how you did pervert the
ancient laws of our Kingdom, sir ...

CHARLES: Cromwell, we have walked
this ground together too often ...
I will not walk it again with you,
sir ... If you have proposals to
make to me ... Make them plainly ...
Without debate ... And I will listen
to them ... and consider my answer ...

        (CROMWELL FIGHTING TO
         MAKE CONTACT WITH THE
         KING, AND SHOW HIM THE
         THE REALITY OF HIS
         WEAKNESS:)

CROMWELL: Before God, I tell you,
sir ... The terms have already been
put to you by the Army, and the
Commons, these ten days past ...
I come to tell you that if you
do not quickly agree to these terms ...
Believe me, sir ... Your life and
soul stand in great mortal danger!

CHARLES: Cromwell ... I am confused ...
There is such a discordant counter-
point of airs ... Now, you would have
me search my heart for the light of
God ... Now, you would force terms
upon me by threat ... I do see you
play strategy with me!

CROMWELL: I beg of you. If you
do not agree with these terms ...
There can be no end to this thing ..
I tell you, but your sure destruction.

CHARLES: Cromwell ... How can any King put his hand to such terms? They would take everything from the King. Command of my army, all money in the kingdom - Law ... Justice ... Everything would be taken from the hand of the King. And they would have me put my hand to the destruction of the old church ... Sir ... A statue would better serve you as King in such a Kingdom!

CROMWELL: Government is but dross and dung compared to God. You should rejoice, sir ... You should thank God that He has granted you this great favour ... To reflect upon and repent your sins ...

    (CHARLES IMPATIENT WITH
     ALL THIS TALK OF SOUL
     AND SIN ... GETTING
     DOWN TO BUSINESS)

CHARLES: You tell me to speak plain. To open my heart to you ... This I will do, sir ... I know what brings you to Windsor ... Your friends fly your cause ... The army splits into factions ... Honest men run to the country ... you know I am no fool with men. It is clear to me ... If Cromwell comes to Windsor to treat with the King - Cromwell is not strong enough to stand without the King.

CROMWELL: Sir, you read me wrong. Believe me! I come to you in great strength ... There's no man in the three Kingdoms who would put down our cause ... I beg you to believe me when I tell you this.

CHARLES: Then tell me, Cromwell ... What brings you then to Windsor, to speak with a man against whom God has witnessed? (Cont ...)

          (CROMWELL STANDS
           FOR A MOMENT, LOOKING
           AWAY. THIS IS NOT A
           QUESTION HE CAN
           ANSWER DIRECTLY. THE
           LAST PERSON HE IS
           GOING TO ADMIT HIS
           FAILURE TO MAKE
           CONTACT WITH GOD
           WITH IS CHARLES.
           CHARLES WATCHES HIM.
           HE HAS CROMWELL NOW)

CHARLES: (cont) What brings you to
Windsor, then, Cromwell?

(On to next page)

CROMWELL: Sir ... I tell you,
your reading is gravely at fault ...

    (CHARLES WAITS
    FOR THE TRUE
    REASONS.

    CROMWELL SLOWLY
    ARTICULATES HIS
    THOUGHTS,
    WORKING IT OUT,
    AS HE SPEAKS)

I would have a King as a central
authority in the country. There
has been such warring between
authorities these six years,
the people stand in great
confusion.. If we do not quickly
establish a central authority
that can command their obedience
the three kingdoms will fall to
anarchy ...

CHARLES: Then I do read you
right, Cromwell .. Without the
King you cannot stand. You
cannot order the Kingdom.
Without the King, the Kingdom
will dissolve into anarchy ...

CROMWELL: (CONTINUING HIS THOUGHTS)
Yet ... If it proves that the
Judgement of God has turned
against the King ... Then this
is a plain decree from God that
search be made for some other
authority ....

    (CHARLES IS
    IMPATIENT TO
    GET DOWN TO THE
    REAL ISSUE.
    WHAT DOES CROMWELL
    WANT OF CHARLES)

CHARLES: Cromwell .. I am ready
to listen to any words that
might bring peace to the
Kingdom - without dishonour
to any man in the (cont ...)

CHARLES: (cont) making of it.
If you have terms to put to me
- put them plainly ......

CROMWELL: Sir, the temper of
Parliament and the Army is hot.
They will not sell the lives of
all their brothers who fell by
their sides in these years of
war lightly. There can be no
other terms but what has already
been put to you. Neither
Parliament nor Army will accept
anything less than these, sir ...

     (CHARLES IS FURIOUS.
      NOW THAT IT IS
      CLEAR TO HIM THAT
      CROMWELL HAS NOT
      COME TO OFFER ANY
      CONCESSIONS BUT
      TO FRIGHTEN HIM
      INTO CAPITULATION
      THERE IS NO MORE
      HOLDING BACK HIS
      WORDS. HE TURNS
      ON CROMWELL)

CHARLES: Hear me, sir! By no
other way can you divert God's
wrath upon you than by restoring
to God his King. By restoring
to the people their King, sir ...
Such things are their due. You
shall give God his due by
restoring his pure worship and
His true Church. Rightly
regulated, according to His
word, You will put the people
in their rights and liberties
by recovering to them the rule
of the Law and the authority of
the King.

CROMWELL: Sir ...I do swear to you
before God ... The first month
of the New Year will not be
out, and your trial and your
judges will be appointed. I
beg of you ... Pray with me, a
short space ..

CHARLES: (TURNING AWAY) My
architect waits me, Cromwell.
I would leave you to your
prayers.

CROMWELL: Sir ... I beg you ..
Let us go down on our knees
and pray to God, that he will
fill our hearts with His Light
and let us see into the dark
places of our souls ... That he
might help you to the True
Witness he has shown others ...

CHARLES: By your favour,
Cromwell! You weary me with
all this talk of God's Light
and God's Witness .... Sir ..
Have you observed when some
men's conscience cry out
against them and accuse them
for sedition and self interest,
how they stop its mouth with the
name and noise of religion!

CROMWELL: Sir ... There is great
urgency in this ... Kneel and
pray with me.

CHARLES: Their interest is
always made God's ... Their
ambition marches under the
colours of piety ..... You hear
from them the voice of Jacob -
but you feel the hands of Esau!

            (CROMWELL IS
             FIGHTING BACK
             HIS ANGER AT
             THIS ATTACK..
             HE MOVES AWAY
             FROM THE KING)

CROMWELL: By your leave, sir
... I would go apart and pray...

CHARLES: Consider, sir... To
judge my cause by its earthly
success ... My judgement of
things by my earthly misfortunes ...
Is this not the reasonings of a
fleshly man who does reason and
read by flesh alone?

    (CROMWELL IS ON
    HIS KNEES,
    FIGHTING WITH
    HIS TEMPER.

    CHARLES WATCHES
    HIM.

    CROMWELL IS
    TREMBLING WITH
    FURY. HE PRAYS,
    HIS EYES CLOSED,
    FOR THE PEACE OF
    GOD TO RETURN TO
    HIM.

    CHARLES TAKES UP
    A PRAYER BOOK...
    HE HAS NO NEED
    TO COMPOSE HIS
    OWN PRAYERS TO
    GOD. EVERYTHING
    IS SET DOWN IN
    THE PRAYER BOOK
    FOR HIM. HE
    FINDS THE PRAYER
    HE IS LOOKING FOR...
    AND READS IT,
    FACING CROMWELL,
    AND INTONING THE
    PRAYER LIKE A
    PRIEST)

Almighty God, the Father of Our
Lord Jesus Christ, who desireth
not the death of a sinner but
rather that he may turn from
his wickedness...

    (CROMWELL REALISES
    THE PRAYER CHARLES
    IS AIMING AT HIM...
    IT IS THE ABSOLUTION
    OR REMISSION OF SINS...)

CROMWELL: Sir! By your favour!

CHARLES: (IGNORING HIM) But rather that he may turn from his wickedness and live, and hath given power and commandment to His Ministers, to declare and pronounce His people, being penitent, the Absolution and Remission of their sins. He Pardoneth and absolveth all them that truly repent....

(AS THE KING READS, IT SUDDENLY BECOMES CLEAR TO CROMWELL, THAT HIS RAGE IS GOD GIVEN. AGAINST SUCH PERVERSIONS OF THE RELIGION OF GOD, GOD DEMANDS ONLY RAGE - THE RAGE OF MOSES WHO PUT DOWN THE MAKERS OF THE GOLDEN CALF... AND UNDERNEATH THIS THERE IS A DIM AWARENESS THAT HIS WHOLE LIFE RESTS ON THE FOUNDATION WHICH CHARLES CHALLENGES. IF CROMWELL IS NOT ON THE LORD'S SIDE - THEN HIS WHOLE LIFE, SPIRITUAL AND PHYSICAL IS FORFEIT... CHARLES AND CROMWELL HAVE BEEN TRYING TO ARGUE EACH OTHER INTO SPIRITUAL AND PHYSICAL SUICIDE.

CROMWELL RISES... HE HAS MADE CONTACT WITH GOD AGAIN... THE LIGHT OF GOD'S TRUTH IS SHINING IN HIS EYES. (cont ...)

CROMWELL: Thy will be done!

                         HE GOES TO THE
                         KING..KNEELS..
                         AND KISSES HIS
                         HAND)

CROMWELL: By your leave, sir.
I will not keep you from your
architect.. God's Will be done,
sir...

CHARLES: Amen, General....
No man can hold back its
execution.

                    (CROMWELL GOES
                     OUT INTO THE
                     CORRIDOR.
                     HIS HEAD IS HIGH.
                     HE IS FULL OF
                     REJOICING THAT
                     THE SPIRIT OF
                     GOD HAS RETURNED
                     TO HIM. HE IS
                     ALREADY COMPOSING
                     THE SPEECH IN
                     HIS MIND FOR
                     PARLIAMENT)

4.   INT.   THE CORRIDOR.

                    (SHOT OF CROMWELL
                     WALKING THROUGH THE
                     CORRIDORS OF THE
                     CASTLE, OUT INTO
                     THE COURTYARD
                     AGAINST THE VOICE
                     OF CROMWELL:)

CROMWELL: (V.O.) Mr. Speaker...
If any man had carried the
design of deposing the King
and disinheriting his posterity
- or if any man had yet such
a design, he should (cont ...)

CROMWELL: (V.O.) be the greatest
traitor and rebel in the world...
But since the providence of God
has cast this upon us, I can not
but submit to Providence...
I would pray to God to bless
our Council, and do with the
King, according to God's will...

(FINAL SHOT OF
 CROMWELL WALKING
 THROUGH THE
 COURTYARD..)

FADE OUT

SECTION THREE

SECTION THREE
PRODUCING THE PLAY
PRODUCER'S NOTES
by INNES LLOYD, Producer, THIRTY MINUTE THEATRE

One of the first decisions a Drama Producer has to make is what sort of plays he wants to put on. This is bound to reflect his feelings about Drama — about Society — about the dramatically exploitable situations in the human predicament, and the material that is available. I believe that if he hasn't got a personal attitude to the sort of work he is doing, an inconsistency of style and content will be apparent in the finished product.

To do this it is essential to search for a quality of writing, of direction and of acting which one believes will excite or stimulate or entertain an audience. But the play or idea is the springboard where it all starts.

To help him select and evaluate scripts, the Television Producer works with a Script Editor. Occasionally the initial contact is between the Author and Script Editor. This was the case with Cecil P. Taylor's trilogy REVOLUTION. After preliminary meetings, the idea of three plays about Cromwell, Lenin and Castro were put to me as Producer of THIRTY MINUTE THEATRE for inclusion in the 1970 Season.

CROMWELL would basically deal with a secret confrontation with Charles I at Windsor — a confrontation where Cromwell pleads in the Lord's name that Charles will recognise the authority of Parliament.

The dramatic conflict in 'Lenin' concerned an argument between Lenin and Zinoviev prior to a session of the Central Committee of the Bolsheviks. During the argument, Lenin shows a ruthless dedication and intention to power-drive the Central Committee into agreeing that a violent uprising against the ruling Government is the only road left open to them. The argument won; the October Revolution followed.

In the third play, we trace Castro and his followers from the day of their landing in Cuba, 3rd December 1956, till Christmas Day when they have battled against the elements, Baptista's forces, and informers to reach Pico Turquino, the highest mountain in Cuba.

In a previous THIRTY MINUTE THEATRE season a trilogy about Hitler, Mussolini and Stalin under the title of THESE MEN ARE DANGEROUS had received an enthusiastic audience and press reaction. Therefore the idea of another trilogy in this vein was a good one. It would take a perceptive look at three giants of history who had, or in the case of Castro is having, a profound and drastic influence throughout the world. The overall title decided upon was REVOLUTION.

The finances of mounting a television play are another factor one has to bear in mind when buying a script. In this case, CROMWELL and LENIN had small casts and would be able to accommodate much of the heavy financial outlay of CASTRO which had a large cast and an ambitious design problem.

Having decided to buy the trilogy, the next process for me as Producer was to pick Directors for each of the plays. Their part in the process of getting the play to the screen was crucial. — Firstly they had to be Directors who would interpret honestly the intention of the Author, and secondly, they needed to be Directors who were enthusiastic and in sympathy with the plays.

The Director in Television is akin to the Director in films. The Producer decides which Director he wants, and offers him a script. When the Director has accepted it, he sets in motion the machinery which is necessary to bring a production to the screen. At this stage the Producer and Director will discuss what money is available for the facilities required, whom they are going to cast, and the Director will hold design, costume, make-up and technical planning meetings. At these meetings he will outline his ideas about how he believes the play should be shot — what the mood of the play is — talk about the period and the design which he feels would be right for it — about the actors' physical characteristics and how it might affect make-up — decide on the camera mountings which will permit him to manoeuvre so that he can get maximum visual impact — and he will discuss any particular sound effects which might be required. At each of these meetings he deals with experts in their own field who will also contribute their ideas. A television production is a team effort with all the contributions, either artistic or mechanical, being co-ordinated and manipulated by the Director.

The Producer's role, once the production is in the process of working up — and in the case of THIRTY MINUTE THEATRE this takes four weeks — is to stand aside, emerging only if his advice is sought, or if he feels that things are happening which don't tally with his original conception. During the rehearsal period the Producer joins the Author and Script Editor at the first read through. Two days before going into the studio he attends a run through, and on the day of the recording he watches the programme being put together. His notes of production points or performances are discussed with the Director before the final recording. To have an objective eye that has not lived with a production throughout has been proved to be an effective yardstick.

To return to the trilogy. In REVOLUTION, three problems of casting occurred. To pick actors who could, within the stretch of imagination, eventually have the physical characteristics of Lenin, or Castro and Che Guevara. The Lenin of our play was a Lenin in disguise — a wig, and at this stage no beard. It was also important to find an actor of strength who could communicate the revolutionary zeal and ruthlessness of Lenin. I think we achieved this in casting Lee Montague, and Norman Rossington complemented him as Zinoviev. Castro was some six foot five inches, and had to contrast in height and temperament with Che Guevara — here again, Bernard Horsfall as Castro and Tom Conti as Che Guevara fulfilled the physical specifications, and at the same time were actors who had the range and experience needed to play these parts. With Cromwell and Charles I, it was important to find the right chemistry in the actors, and we picked Leslie Sands and Kenneth Colley, both of whom are actors of distinction.

Building a jungle and giving a realistic impression of the mountain top of Pico Turquino presented the designer, Stuart Walker, with a challenge. I suppose one of the hardest design problems is to build within the confines of a studio set, and make it look natural, the sort of background which would make the Castro story appear authentic.

In any television production, creative energies are unleashed. There are moments of frustration, moments of excitement, at times compromises are essential but overall there is a sense of adventure and purpose.

The Writer must know what he wants to say — the Producer must know what he wants to buy — the Director must know how he will interpret the story — and the actors must have an instinct for what they are interpreting. When all these factors are working together, one hopes that the energy and electricity of Drama is communicated to the audience.

BRITISH BROADCASTING CORPORATION

TELEVISION CENTRE   WOOD LANE   LONDON   W12

TELEPHONE 01-743 8000   TELEGRAMS BROADCASTS LONDON TELEX

CABLES BROADCASTS LONDON-W1   TELEX 22182

17th October 1969

Dear Cecil,

    I am glad to say that we have found a director for your play 'AT WINDSOR' and he has made a point with which both Innes and myself agree. He feels that it would be better to cut pages 7, 8, 9, 10, 11 and half of 12 after Charles' speech ending; "and be cut down by both sides.", in order to get in to the confrontation between Charles and Cromwell earlier.

    As this script will probably need cutting anyway Innes and I have no objection to this if you have none. Anyway please let me know what you think about it.

    Whilst writing, is there any chance of having the Lenin script next week? As you appreciate these plays have to be set up together and we have now reached the planning stage of the three weeks when we are likely to record them and without a script to show a director we are somewhat stuck.

    Sorry to pressurise you over this but it would be a great help in future planning.

    With all kind regards.

                    Yours sincerely,

                    Derek Hoddinott
                    Script Editor
                THIRTY MINUTE THEATRE

73

DIRECTOR'S NOTES
by TRISTAN DE VERE COLE

On reading the draft, I seem to remember thinking the following: (1.) It read very well. (2.) Did such a meeting take place? (3.) It was obviously too long. (This referring to first draft.) (4.) For a play about Cromwell, there was a remarkable emphasis on Charles. (The play was originally titled CROMWELL.)

I proposed a number of cuts and rehashing of scenes so that we got to the confrontation as soon as possible. Rather to my surprise and pleasure, the playwright agreed to these without a murmur.

The detail and research in the script was evident and although bits of the dialogue were fascinating, there was a danger of some of them intruding and raising too many irrelevant questions in the audience's mind, i.e. the story of Cromwell and Charles fighting as children. (In the first draft.)

It was obviously a play that was in danger of being melodramatic but, if played with conviction, could be most exciting. Being costume and period, one had a better chance of getting away with it — the play itself being a bit of a 'theatrical' piece.

As a generalisation, script, casting and production are, I believe, a Director's priority. In casting, one had a certain amount of leeway with Cromwell — conflicting portraits and descriptions — perhaps a general impression in the public's mind of a 'solid' man. With Charles, however, the public have a firm 'Van Dyke' image and I felt strongly we should adhere to this.

I was very happy that Leslie Sands was very keen to do it. In my letter to him, I suggested he should play it as 'sent' as possible. This, in conjunction with his own physical force and 'Ironside's' face, I felt, would make a splendid Cromwell.

Although only 32, I was confident Kenneth Colley could take the necessary make up and, apart from looking remarkably like Charles, I felt he could 'act' him. (One of my faults, in the eyes of friends, was that I did not make him arrogant or proud enough. Having settled to play the public's image of Charles, I think, perhaps, this is fair comment.

In rehearsal, we spent a fair amount of time chatting and it was interesting that although neither actor was selfish, they were obviously getting immersed in their own characters. Leslie's approach was more 'defined' from the start. Kenneth relied very much on 'sorting things out' before he could get to grips with Charles, and we had considerable discussions on Charles' state of mind.

The designer and I went to Windsor to research — had splendid day but didn't glean much of use from the most helpful Royal Librarian. Charles' apartments and Chapel would have been built by Edward Third and we decided to base our sets on that period, with Stuart overtones.

I also visited Kensington Gardens Museum where I got the idea of Charles having a watch. I also thought that Charles' dogs sould be something an audience could latch on to.

Because of my Design Plan, I obviously had worked out my shots before rehearsal and they were substantially the same on the take. But I certainly didn't inhibit the actors and indeed we tried a number of variations.

I had set the sound and lighting a considerable number of problems by wanting to shoot 360 degrees. These they surmounted with a minimum of fuss.

The opening caption, I hoped would set the religious fanatical views of Cromwell — Cromwell with his troops at Dunbar against the Lord's Prayer from the 1643 Soldier's Bible.

HERE FOLLOWS A REPRODUCTION OF THE
BEGINNING AND END OF THE DIRECTOR'S CAMERA
SCRIPT

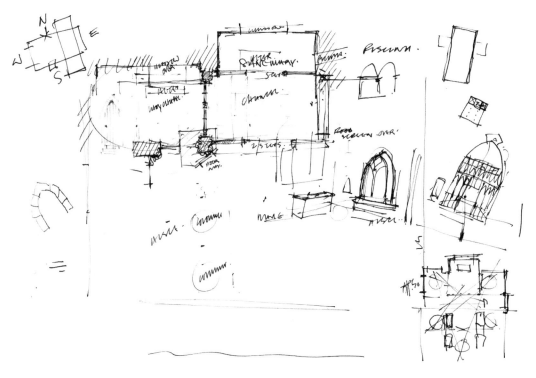

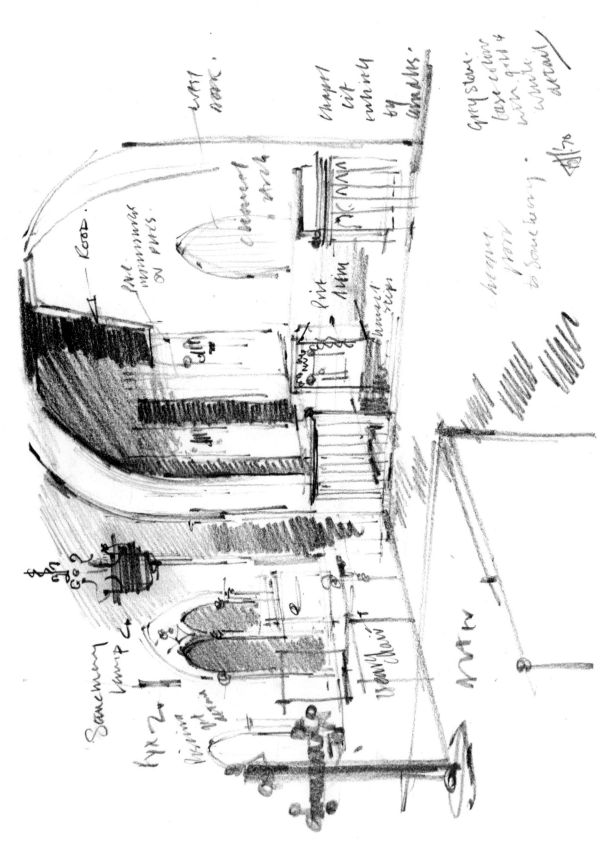

Directors sketch for set.

APPENDIX

TELEVISION MARKETS

B.B.C. Television
Television Centre
Wood Lane, W.12

Granada Television
36 Golden Square
London, W.1

Thames Television, Ltd.
Teddington Lock
Teddington, Middlesex

Yorkshire Television
Television Centre
Leeds, LS3 1JS

A.T.V., Elstree Studios
Eldon Avenue
Boreham Wood, Herts.

London Weekend Television
Station House
Harrow Road
Wembley, Middlesex

Writers who intend seriously writing for television are recommended to join THE WRITERS GUILD OF GREAT BRITAIN, as Associate Members. The Guild publish a monthly bulletin about markets and advise members on such matters as reputable agents, minimum fees and terms of contracts, etc . . The address is:—
WRITERS' GUILD OF GREAT BRITAIN
430 Edgeware Road
LONDON, W.2

POSTSCRIPT

The playwright is not the one man band the novelist, short story writer or poet is. A play needs much more than a writer and reader for it to happen.

I hope I have made clear in what I have written that whatever was achieved in screening CHARLES AND CROMWELL was not a one man achievement. The Producer, Script Editor, Director and actors all contributed to a deeper realisation of the theme of the play. As in all happy productions, the result was bigger than the script.

This is no expression of modesty or humility. I believe I did a good job of work on the play. But I am conscious of how much I leaned on the talents and abilities of everyone involved in the production and how well they served the script.

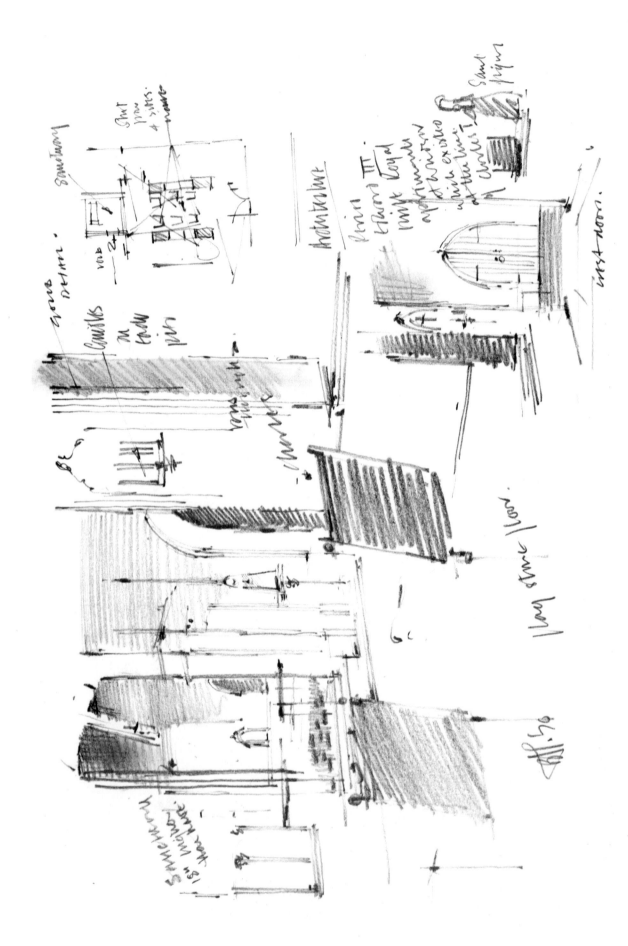

Directors sketch for set.

CAMERA SCRIPT

COMMON ABBREVIATIONS USED IN CAMERA SCRIPT

BCU. — Big Close-up. (Showing head or part of the head.)

CU. — Close-up. (Showing head and shoulders.)

MCU. — Medium close-up. (Showing subject just above waist.)

CMS. — Close medium shot. (Cutting the subject below the waist.)

M.S. — Medium shot. (Cutting subject at the knees.)

MLS. — Medium long shot. (Showing full-length figure.)

LS. — Long shot. (Figure about half height of the screen.)

VLS. — Very long shot. (Showing full set.)

O.S. — Overscene. (Speech, music or sound effects over picture when their source is not visible.)

O.S.V. — Off-screen voice. (Voice of person heard but not seen.)

O.O.V. — Out of vision. (Speech, music, effects heard but source unseen.)

A.B. — As before. (Camera has exactly the same shot as immediately before.)

Grams. — Music or sound effects from gramophone records.

Cam. — Camera.

Mic. — Microphone.

F/X — Sound effects on tape or disk.

Spot, F/X — Sound effects made in studio.

V.T.R. — Video tape recording. (Recording on magnetic tape of vision and sound. The actual recording of the play.)

THIRTY MINUTE THEATRE: "REVOLUTION - CROMWELL" by CECIL P. TAYLOR

PAGE	SHOTS	SCENE/CHARACTERS	D/N	CAMS/BOOMS
1		TK.1 Opening Titles		
1	1 – 5	1. INT. THE KING'S PRIVATE CHAPEL, WINDSOR CASTLE OLIVER CROMWELL + TJ. Slides 1 – 3 + Caption	D	2 Caption 1A 3A,4A 3B B1 A1
2	6 – 23	2. INT. THE KING'S PRIVATE APARTMENT, WINDSOR CASTLE KING CHARLES I THOMAS HERBERT + two dogs	D	3C,2A,2B 4B Fish A2
		R E C O R D I N G B R E A K		
6	24 – 102	3. INT. THE CHAPEL CROMWELL CHARLES	D	1B 1C,4A,2E Fish B1 4C,2C,2D,3D,3E A1
		R E C O R D I N G B R E A K		
28	103	4. INT. THE CORRIDOR CROMWELL	D	2F 2A Fish
	104	+ Roller Caption		1 Roller

thirty minute theatre

"Cromwell"

by Cecil P. Taylor

TELECINE ONE   /S.O.F./
Standard Opening Titles   (Dur: 13")

        MIX
1.   2 (lurk)   /   SOUND
           WS Caption   1643 Lord's
           Slow tighten   Prayer
                                                   Jingle of
                                                   harness
        SUPER TJ. SLIDE 1   Stamping of
           "REVOLUTION"   horses
                                                   Low wind
        SUPER TJ. SLIDE 2
           "CROMWELL"

        SUPER TJ. SLIDE 3
           "by CECIL P. TAYLOR"

        MIX   /1A 3A,4A 3B/
2.   3 A   /   B1   A1
           Crucifix
           Loosen and   1.   INT. KING'S PRIVATE CHAPEL,
           pull back   WINDSOR CASTLE.
           down aisle   28th DECEMBER, 1648
           to door
        /END POS. B/   Carry over
                                              Lord's Prayer
           Let Cromwell's
           back in R.   (CAM. ON THE CHRIST ON
                                  CRUCIFIX ON THE ALTAR.

                                  MOVE BACK TO SHOW THE
                                  ALTAR, THEN THE WHOLE
                                  CHAPEL.

                                  HOLD ON THE DOORWAY,
3.   4 A   AS CROMWELL ENTERS.
           MCU Cromwell
    2   Loosen and   HE STANDS FOR A MOMENT,
      CAPT pan him L.   THEN UNCOVERS HIS HEAD.
           Crab R.   HE LOOKS ROUND THE
   4 A/B   Use b/g pillar   CHAPEL. HE WALKS DOWN
           to frame   TO THE ALTAR AND STUDIES
                                  THE CRUCIFIX. HE STANDS
                                  STUDYING THE FIGURE OF
                                  CHRIST FOR SOME TIME.
4.   1 A   THEN TAKES A GRIP ON
           MCU Cromwell   HIMSELF. HE TURNS HIS
                                  BACK ON THE ALTAR AND
                                  THE OTHER RELICS OF
5.   3 B   ON TURN   PAPACY. HE THROWS HIMSELF
           LS Cromwell   ON HIS KNEES TO PRAY)
           Slow push in
           to CU

        (CAM 2 NEXT)

                          - 1 -

(ON CAM 3)

CROMWELL: Dear God in Heaven, who searcheth our hearts and knoweth all things that lie buried in all men, You only are worthy to be feared and trusted and Your appearance patiently waited upon. You will not fail your people.

(CAMERA ON HIS FACE. HE IS STRAINING, FIGHTING TO REACH OUT TO GOD)

/2 into 'A'/

Dear God, guide me in this thing you have put upon me, Lord. Dear God I am beset with fleshy reasoning. Help me to recover your Presence that has withdrawn from me these three months ... Dear God give me some sign, that I can speak as in Your name to this man ... Help me to accomplish that work which will be for the good of this Kingdom and all its people ...

(FADE VOICE)

6. 2 A _____/
    LS Charles
    with dogs
                              /3C, 2A, 2B 4B/
    . Hold his   /Fish   A2/
    rise and
    move L.   2. INT. THE KING'S PRIVATE APARTMENT.

                              (CAMERA ON CHARLES'
                              ANGRY FACE. HE IS
                              RINGING HIS SILVER
                              BELL, IMPATIENTLY, FOR
                              HIS ATTENDANT, THOMAS
7. 4 B   HERBERT.
    MS entrance
    Let Herbert in   HERBERT RUSHES IN AND
8. 2 A   ON LOOK Bow ? BOWS TO THE KING)
    2-S Herbert/
    Charles   HERBERT: Sir?

                       CHARLES: Sir, I have been
                       ringing that bell these five
9. 4 B   minutes!/
    MCU Herbert

    (CAM 2 NEXT)   - 2 -

10.	2 A	
		MCU Charles

HERBERT: I was with Colonel Whichcott, sir. He called me to him./

Pan him R. to sit in MS

| 11. | 4 B | |
| | | Deep 2-S Herbert/Charles |

CHARLES: By your favour, Herbert! If Whichcott would speak to my attendants, he must first ask your freedom from me, sir. I am still King, Herbert!/

(HERBERT BOWS HIS APOLOGY)

Did we not appoint this after-noon for a meeting with our architect?

HERBERT: This we did, sir.

CHARLES: At this hour, Herbert? Three hours after noon?

HERBERT: Mr. Webb is here, sir. ~~This is the business upon which the Governor called~~ me. The Colonel —/

| 12. | 2 A | |
| | | MCU Charles |

CHARLES: What delays him? There is much work to be done. This afternoon, we are to consider the facade of the new palace at Whitehall./

| 13. | 4 B | |
| | | MCU Herbert |

HERBERT: Sir ... Colonel Whichcott is entertaining Mr. Webb. He asks your indulgence, sir. Some Divine has come from London. He begs to see you, sir./

| 14. | 2 | |
| | | MCU Charles |

CHARLES: Has Webb brought more drawings with him?/

| 15. | 4 | |
| | | MCU Herbert |

HERBERT. He has, sir. The Divine waits you in the Small Chapel, sir./

| 16. | 2 | |
| | | CU Charles |

(CAM 4 NEXT)

(ON CAM 1)

CHARLES: Consider, sir... To judge my cause by its earthly success... My judgement of things by my earthly misfortunes... In this not the reasonings of a fleshly man who does reason and read by flesh alone?

(CROMWELL IS ONE
HIS KNEES,
FIGHTING WITH
HIS TEMPER.

CHARLES WATCHES
HIM.

CROMWELL IS
TREMBLING WITH
FURY. HE PRAYS?
HIS EYES CLOSED,
FOR THE PEACE OF
GOD TO RETURN TO
HIM.

Let Charles
Cross L. to
deep 2-S
Charles/Cromwell

CHARLES TAKES UP
A PRAYER BOOK...
HE HAS NO NEED
TO COMPOSE HIS
OWN PRAYERS TO
GOD. EVERYTHING
IS SET DOWN IN
THE PRAYER BOOK
FOR HIM. HE
FINDS THE PRAYER
HE IS LOOKING FOR...
AND READS IT?
FACING CROMWELL?
AND INTONING THE
PRAYER LIKE A
PRIEST)

3 — CAP.

1 — A/B.

Almighty God, The Father of Our Lord Jesus Christ, who desireth not the death of a sinner but rather that he may turn from his wickedness...

(CROMWELL REALISES
THE PRAYER CHARLES
IS AIMING AT HIM...
IT IS THE ABSOLUTION
OR REMISSION OF SINS...)

(CAM 2 NEXT)

(ON CAM 1)

CROMWELL: Sir! By Your Favour!

Push in
on Cromwell

CHARLES: (IGNORING HIM) But rather that he may turn from his wickedness and live, and hath goven power and commandment to His Ministers, to declare and pronounce His people, being penitent, the Absolution and Remission of their sins. He Pardoneth and absolveth all them that truly repent....

(AS THE KING READS, IT SUDDENLY BECOMES CLEAR TO CROMWELL, THAT HIS RAGE IS GOD GIVEN. AGAINST SUCH PERVERSIONS OF THE RELIGION OF GOD, GOD EMANDS ONLY RAGE - THE RAGE OF MOSES WHO PUT DOWN THE MAKERS OF THE GOLDEN CALF... AND UNDERNEATH THIS, THERE IS A DIM AWARENESS THAT HIS WHOLE LIFE RESTS ON THE FOUNDATION WHICH CHARLES CHALLENGE. IF CROMWELL IS NOT ON THE LORDS SIDE, - THEN HIS WHOLE LIFE, SPIRITUAL AND PHYSICAL IS FORFEIT... CHARLES AND CROMWELL HAVE BEEN TRYING TO ARGUE EACH OTHER INTO SPIRITUAL AND PHYSICAL SUICIDE.

Loosen on
his rise
include
Charles L.

CROMWELL: Thy will be done ...

(CAM 2 NEXT)

(ON CAM 1)

                                        CROMWELL RISES ...
                                        HE HAS MADE CONTACT
                                        WITH GOD AGAIN ...
                                        THE LIGHT OF GOD'S
                                        TRUTH IS SHINING IN
                                        HIS EYES. HE GOES TO
                                        THE KING .. KNEELS ..
        Crab R.   AND KISSES HIS HAND)
        Cromwell/Charles

                                        CROMWELL: By your leave, sir.
                                        I will not keep you from your
                                        architect ... God's will be
                                        done, sir ...

                                        CHARLES: Amen, General. No man
                                        can hold back its execution.

102.   2 E
        CU Cromwell   (CROMWELL GOES OUT
        Loosen to   INTO THE CORRIDOR.
        include Charles   HIS HEAD IS HIGH.
        Pull back with   HE IS FULL OF
        Cromwell   REJOICING THAT
        Let Cromwell go   THE SPIRIT OF GOD
        R.   HAS RETURNED TO
                                        HIM. HE IS ALREADY
        End LS Charles   COMPOSING THE SPEECH
                                        IN HIS MIND FOR
                                        PARLIAMENT)

        RECORDING BREAK   Set Corridor

-----

103.   2 A (back)
          MS Cromwell
          Track back
          with him   4.   INT.   THE CORRDIOR.   DAY.

                                       (SHOT OF CROMWELL
                                       WALKING THROUGH THE
                                       CORRIDORS OF THE
          SUPER   CASTLE, AGAINST THE
104.   1   VOICE OF CROMWELL)
          Roller Caption:

          CROMWELL   CROMWELL: Mr. Speaker ...
          by CECIL P. TAYLOR   If any man had carried the
                                   design of deposing the King
                                   and disinheriting his
          Cromwell   posterity - then he would
          LESLIE SANDS   be the greatest traitor
                                   and rebel in the world.
          Charles   But since the providence of
          KENNETH COLLEY   God has cast this upon us,
                                   I cannot but submit to
          Thomas Herbert   Providence. I would pray
          DAVYD HARRIES   to God to bless our council
                                   and do with the King
                                   according to God's will ...
          Costumes
          ELIZABETH WALLER

          Make-up
          MARGARET MACKINNON

          Lighting
          HOWARD KING

          Sound
          GORDON MACKIE

          Designer
          BRIAN TREGIDDEN

          Script Editor
          DEREK HODDINOTT

          Producer
          INNES LLOYD

          Directed by
          TRISTAN de VERE COLE
          BBC-tv

                    FADE SOUND & VISION

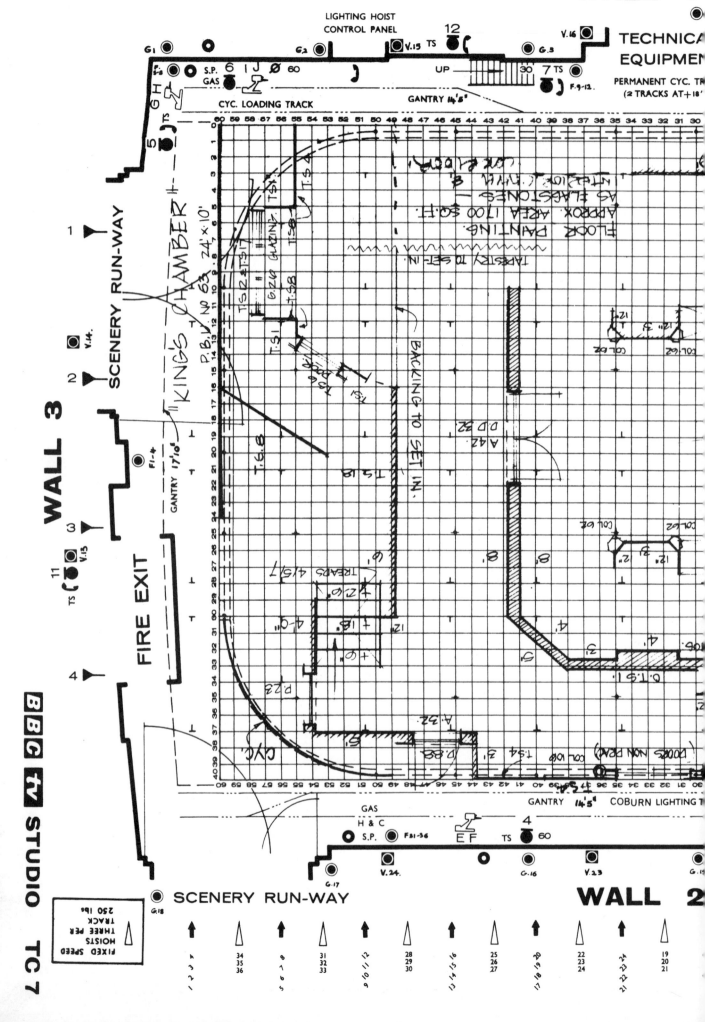